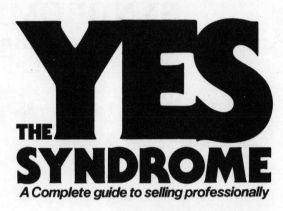

THE YES SYNDROME

A Complete guide to selling professionally

by Don Beveridge

THE YES SYNDROME
A complete guide to selling professionally

by
D.W. (Don) Beveridge, Jr.

A 'professionals' book selection and in the library of 'Business Leaders.'

Printed in the United States of America

NOTICE

If you want to sell
your product to our
company, be sure your
product is accompanied by
a plan, which will
so help our business
that we will be more
anxious to buy than
you are to sell.

D. W. Beveridge, Jr.
and Associates

P O BOX 123 BARRINGTON ILLINOIS 60010

MANAGEMENT AND MARKETING CONSULTANTS

THE PROFESSIONAL EDGE

An outstanding audio-workbook, self training series complete and in-depth as narrated by DON BEVERIDGE.

The skills of the professional salesperson are profiled as a system for selling in the "MAKING CUSTOMERS WANT TO BUY" edition. The techniques of skilled sales management are detailed in the management edition, "HOW TO LEAD AND MOTIVATE."

Each of these self-teaching, programmed-learning-type libraries contain six audio cassettes on twelve vital subjects plus an in-depth workbook manual complete with checklists, tools, quiz reviews, illustrations and "How To Do It" details.

 Your needs may be for the sales or sales management programs or perhaps both. In any case they provide an opportunity to improve skills and improve your effectiveness immediately.

These training systems may be ordered by designating your choice of either "SALES" or "MANAGEMENT" programs and sending your check for $150.00 each program to:

Beveridge Business Systems
P.O. Box 223
Barrington, IL 60010

DON BEVERIDGE 'SPEAKS OUT'

Live excerpts from actual DON BEVERIDGE convention presentations with all the excitement and motivation of being there.

"ENSURING A UNIQUE COMPETITIVE ADVANTAGE"....a presentation to the salespeople of the American Machine Tool Distributors Association.

"PERFORMANCE, PRODUCTIVITY AND STANDARDS" a presentation to the Textile Rental Association of America to assist managers to establish a 'benchmark' for implementing MBO concepts.

"CHARACTERISTICS OF MOST GOOD MANAGERS" for the National Food Brokers Association providing a management checklist for improved supervisory skills.

"THE SUPERMAN SYNDROME"...delegation is the message for Beatrice Foods Corporation and presented in the unique DON BEVERIDGE style.

two cassettes, four programs
in library binder

This audio cassette series may be purchased by sending $25.00 to:

Beveridge Business Systems
P.O. Box 223
Barrington, IL 60010

Designate "SPEAKS OUT" as your selection.

THE YES SYNDROME

This book is dedicated to my father, now deceased, Don Beveridge, Sr. who was a master salesman and who shared with me his skill beginning at age fourteen.

"EVERYONE LIVES BY SELLING SOMETHING"

Robert Louis Stevenson

Important note:

The format of this book has been designed in a way to facilitate its use as both a textbook and/or a workbook. Sufficient space has been provided for your notes. USE IT!!

PREFACE

The author is appreciative of having had the opportunity for ten years to teach 'systems marketing' and sales management in the continuing education department of the University of Wisconsin. A special appreciation is expressed to Professor William Stillwell and Professor Dick Berry for all the information and knowledge this environment provided.

An individual who initially found difficulty penetrating the author's "gray matter" with the concept of a "customer needs orientation" versus the "product pitch" is also a major contributor in concept to this volume. Mr. Jack Quigley, Chairman of the Board of F.W. Means and Company, as my "boss," finally was effective in showing me "the light."

To the countless salespeople who, for over ten years, two days each week, for twenty weeks each year, provided us the opportunity to do the on-the-job research...to the salesmen in Perth, Australia to selling individuals in Dijon, France; Bristol, England; Malmo, Sweden...to the field representatives in all fifty states of the United States whose names and companies are too numerous to list...a special thanks. This book is about you.

Finally to my wife who for twenty-seven years has always been supportive of whatever it is I do.

D.W.B., Jr.

Chicago, Illinois
June 1982

CONTENTS

THE YES SYNDROME
by
Don Beveridge

ILLUSTRATIVE
INCIDENTS
and EXAMPLES

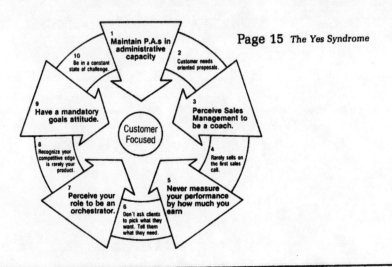

Chicago Tribune

Salesmen fare poorly in survey

EVER SLAM THE DOOR in the face of a salesman? You're not alone, according to Marketing News, a publication of the American Marketing Association. A survey of 10,000 buyers "has documented a tremendous lack of effectiveness and professionalism among the U.S. salesforce." For example, 63 per cent said they wouldn't buy from the same salesman again because of neglect and indifference on the part of salesmen. Eighty-five per cent said the salesman lacked "empathy," and 89 per cent said he didn't know his product.

INTRODUCTION

Recognize that of every ten people functioning as a sales representative only three of each ten actually started with an objective to be in sales!

Arnold Kuthy, Executive V.P. of the George Kistler Company, Allentown, Pennsylvania, suggests that,

"Many salespeople are former coaches with losing seasons, teachers who couldn't spell, liberal arts graduates or dropouts from other careers that 'just didn't work out'."

If true, it's a sincere indictment from one who prides himself on first being himself a "salesperson" and second a very skilled, competent, operational manager.

"...the most accurate evaluation of the selling skills of most salespeople is that they are only fair to adequate."

Mac Rand, Director of Purchasing for Union Carbide, himself a veteran of several decades as a sales rep, in 1980 suggested that of all the salespersons selling to his firm the most accurate evaluation of their skills and abilities would be only "fair to adequate".

Again, an individual who knows selling, and is himself a salesperson suggests the need for improved selling skills is paramount.

We can view the facts in two different ways much as the two shoe salespeople disembarking at the port of a developing nation in Africa perceived them. The first sales representative even before stepping on the soil of this emerging country exclaimed;

"This is terrible, no one here wears shoes...look, nine of ten go barefoot ...what in the world am I doing here?"

Our first salesperson reboards his flight and awaits transportation to a new city he feels will have more and better prospects for his products.

The second salesperson at the same time, in the same city, with the same product steps off and enthusiastically exclaims;

"...the objective is to obtain in the eyes of the buyer an identity of PROBLEM SOLVER."

"Wow, what an opportunity, what potential...NOBODY wears shoes! EVERYONE'S a prospect...*all* have needs I can satisfy".

We feel the fact that most salespeople have selling skills that are only "fair to adequate" is OPPORTUNITY. Opportunity for those salespeople who are willing to accept the disciplines of sales, use a "system of selling" (which makes one professional) and to attain in the eyes of the buyer an image of "problem solver" rather than that of "peddler", is an exceptional opportunity and an opportunity that exists today and will continue to exist for a long, long time.

For generations sales representatives have been identified in the eyes of many as "fast-talking, hard-drinking, joke-telling, car-driving, expense-account-oriented peddlers."

Some are.

Most wish they were not.

Many are not.

This negative identity is a problem of not only the individual salesperson but of his company as well. Many company sales training programs do more to continue such a poor self-image than they do to help correct it.

Here's proof.

When speaking before any group tell them you're going to verbally quickly identify four different sales types by briefly describing industries or companies and ask for their immediate response in terms of "YEA" or "Boooo" relative to how they see, perceive, or feel

Many company sales training programs do more to continue a poor self-image than they do to help correct it.

"SALESPEOPLE CAN BE DIVIDED
INTO THREE GROUPS: THOSE WHO MAKE THINGS
HAPPEN, THOSE WHO WATCH THINGS HAPPEN,
AND THOSE WHO WONDER WHAT HAPPENED."
—John W. Newbern

*Professional sales
people utilize a system
of selling that
emphasizes satisfying
customer needs*

about the professionalism of each selling style or type.

Ready?

Begin by offering "door-to-door encyclopedia salesmen".

Ninety percent of the response will be "boooo".

Next suggest "door-to-door vacuum cleaner salesmen".

The response will be the same.

Now try Xerox salespeople, then offer IBM salespeople and you'll find the image to be a loud "YEA".

Why? Because in most cases the first two sales types are PRODUCT-ORIENTED peddlers who themselves are products of sales training programs which have an emphasis on product knowledge or "closing skills". In the case of Xerox or IBM sales type, they are professionals, utilizing a "system of selling", which emphasizes, satisfying customer needs, and they are products of sales training programs where the emphasis is on the identification and satisfaction of the *customers'* needs...profitably, type skills.

The objective of this book is to help you

play (sell) in their league.

GENERATIONS OF SELLING SKILLS I

PART I

GENERATIONS OF SELLING SKILLS

'THE COMMERCIAL VISITOR'

All individuals engaged in selling and as well the attitudes about salespeople by those who do not sell, can be classified in four levels of competency.

The four generations of selling skills.

Typically referred to as the four generations of sales types, this classification system involves an evolutionary process in which only nine percent of all salespersons evolve to the professional, desired third or fourth generation level. Selling skill levels which are characteristic of the most productive salespeople.

The evolutionary process has other distinguishing characteristics. Novice salespeople historically in their early years of selling migrate to the smaller, less sophisticated, less demanding kinds of prospects. These clients require fewer professional selling skills. A "dropping by" sales call is acceptable where appointments are standard in more sophisticated accounts.

A wholly oral sales presentation would be tolerated where a larger firm would require written proposals and/or visual

"...only nine percent of all people who sell evolve in their selling skills to the professional level."

PROBLEM AREAS FOR SALESPEOPLE

MANAGING TIME AND TERRITORY 60%*

**Percentages are the numbers of all respondents listing the area as a problem

aids.

Factually, for many salespeople at this level there is a fear, an inborn resistance to even ask for the order. Their skill, their technique is so internally motivated...to satisfy their needs, to meet their company's needs...that a subconscious resistance to asking for the order is constantly in evidence. In some cases if these individuals have what they consider a more professional background or education...engineering, science, banking, etc "...often the resistance to ask for the sale can be identified as a feared loss of status, prestige or image to the salesperson." Someone might actually perceive him to be, actually consider him to be a *salesman!* These individuals rest squarely at the first generation of selling skills, a level where approximately forty percent of all sales representatives function.

Factually only about three of ten salespeople began their careers with the objective of being a sales representative. Most started or desired other careers that just "didn't work out." The Josten's Corporation of Minnesota, marketers of recognition products including the National Football League's Super Bowl winners' rings, are often wrongly described as having a sales force of former coaches, the majority of which had losing seasons. In any event, the largest majority of salespeople today did not begin with the intent to be in selling.

Beveridge Business Systems, a Barrington, Illinois sales/marketing consulting firm in the late 1970's surveyed at a client's request the lack of selling successes they were experiencing with "cat scanners." At the time "computed tomography" in the form of "cat scanners" was the most sophisticated x-ray like equipment available to hospitals and radiologists. The client's product from a technological and performance point of view was equal to that of the many competitors. They, however, were dead last in the sales of the units.

The consultant's activities included working in the field with the client's very professional and well educated sales representatives. Some were engineers, others were persons with science backgrounds, pre-med or even a physicist or two. Consciously the sales

"...the largest majority of the world's salespeople did not begin with the intent to be in selling. It's an alternative career."

PROBLEM AREAS FOR SALESPEOPLE

PROSPECTING FOR NEW BUSINESS 43%

First generation salespeople mistakenly perceive selling to be developing close, personal, emotional relationships with the buyer.

calls were loyally and dependably carried out, however, it was quickly noted that in almost every case the closing technique was most often.

"Call us if you need anything," in one form or another.

Subconsciously these "professionals" were highly resistive of asking for the sale. Deep in their "gut" was the fear that if they aggressively requested the order, why, the customer may perceive them to be "salesmen." A definite loss of prestige and status from their point of view. The problem was corrected and the client in 1981 was number two in the world in the sale of "cat scanners" but the salespeople were in fact *commercial visitors*" in their selling skills initially.

This generation of selling skill is identified as the COMMERCIAL VISITOR level and is recognized by one or more of the following criteria.

First, a COMMERCIAL VISITOR in most cases has an emphasis on, and is desirous of, close, personal, emotional relationships with their clients.

It's an antiquated selling ability but many still utilize the technique.

Their emphasis, the salespersons intent, is to "make the buyer like me," and to become personally involved. They place heavy emphasis on antiquated gift giving, Christmas presents, theater or sports tickets. They entertain the secretary, send gifts to the family. This COMMERCIAL VISITOR type sales representative believes subconsciously that he will secure the order because the client eventually feels the business is "owed" to the representative.

Having an awareness of the prospect's personal facts is good business. An occasional lunch or social activity has value. However, when as in the case of the COMMERCIAL VISITOR it relates closely to the reason for the sale, this first generation salesperson is exceptionally vulnerable to competitive sales personnel who are in the third or fourth generation selling skills level. Close emotional relationships as *the reason* for a sale are again, very antiquated selling skills.

There is a second indicator of a COMMERCIAL VISITOR sales type and it is his tendency to "whittle the territory down to the good ole boys." Factually

"...first generation sales types are especially vulnerable to price and specification competitive advantages."

"'Commercial Visitors' have a tendency to whittle the territory down to the 'good-ole boys.'"

these reps are on a consistent, unchanging, dependable routing system; an unchallenging routing system. Years ago when the door-to-door delivery of dairy products was done by the use of a horse and wagon, there was only minimal concern on the part of the dairy company of losing the route salesman himself.

Their real fear was that they would lose the horse!

People who recall or had witnessed this distribution system tell of how the horse would stop automatically at the intended delivery door. The horse would, from habit, pass by those homes where milk was never delivered. The milk route salesman at that time simply made delivery where the horse stopped. The greatest difficulty it would seem would have been to add or drop an account and to re-educate the horse to the new customer list.

This second indicator of a COMMERCIAL VISITOR relates to a similar selling style. The salesperson has simply whittled down the territory to the point he is on a habitual routing system. Few wholly new accounts are solicited or sold. The

PROBLEM AREAS FOR SALESPEOPLE

SELLING AGAINST COMPETITION
43%

salesperson, because of the repetition and lack of challenge in the territory, begins to become dissatisfied or even bored in their job. Their product mix sales are limited and typically it is the competitor who is securing the newer growth customers.

A professional salesperson by design, by plan, drops accounts annually so that they may add new customers with more potential. Their territory is in a continuous evolutionary state.

Whittling the territory down to the "good ole boys" is characteristic of COMMERCIAL VISITORS, in fact their "closing" techniques or skills are most akin to statements such as, "call me if you need anything," and that request is offered consistently to the same clientele.

Finally the COMMERCIAL VISITOR is very desirous of being measured by their *activities* and not their results.

The first generation sales type relates well to "call reports," the laborious, repetitive listing of where the salesperson has been, (which are generally of questionable value*) because they have a format for emphasizing the numbers of calls made rather than their actual sales pro-

What percentage of your time have you targeted for calling on wholly new accounts?

Poorer performing salespeople are desirous of being measured by their activities and not their results.

*See chapter STANDARDS OF PROFESSIONAL SALESPERSONS.

ductivity. They are at times zealously loyal and always at the ready for "other duties"...special assignments which free them momentarily from actually selling. Such a circumstance provides even more *activities* which they can offer as results.

The individuals will verbally detail the huge number of hours they work weekly, they'll be the first to arrive at the office or on the job and the last to leave. It would not be uncommon for the COMMERICAL VISITOR to proudly boast that they haven't taken all their earned vacation for years. Subconsciously this sales rep craves measurements and recognition that are in the activity arena rather than in the sales productivity area.

The story is told of a firm's President calling his sales/marketing consultant who had been on retainer to the company for some time. The client officer was livid having spot-checked some of his sales department's reporting and discovering one of their salespeople who was averaging only two calls a day. In a rage the president called the consultant and demanded,

PROBLEM AREAS FOR SALESPEOPLE

CLOSING MORE EFFECTIVELY
38%

"You better fly over here today" the President insisted. "We've been paying you your fee for years and look at the results. It's a disaster."

The consultant promised immediate action, however, prior to ending the conversation asked of the President,

"Can you tell me any more about this particular sales rep?"

The President hesitated, then said,

"Why yes...he's also our top producer!"

After a long pause of discovery, the consultant made his point and cancelled the crisis trip to see the client by saying,

"Maybe you ought to cut him down to only one call a day!"

It has long been established as counter productive to dictate numbers-of-calls per day. Selling techniques and skills vary which suggest different quantities of calls produce like results in any given sales group.

Forty percent of all salespeople function in such a way as to measure activities and not results. Their career in selling can be considered to be at a skill level a salesperson should progress beyond after only

It has long been established as counter productive for sales management to dictate number-of-calls a day. You cannot legislate productivity.

 eighteen to twenty-four months of sales experience. Unfortunately like the President of the company just described many managers are equally uninformed and they, too, place the primary emphasis on reporting and measuring activities and not the results.

If the evolutionary process does not take place to a more sophisticated selling style, a career in a field other than selling should be seriously considered by such a salesperson . . . and that's also a fact.

THE
PEDDLER

One does not have to be with a company long before they are attending their first sales meeting. This communicating format has component parts that go well beyond the meeting subjects themselves. At coffee breaks or at after meeting cocktails one generally comes across the salesperson who is verbally finding fault with the company message, the products, or the management policies being discussed. This person awaits his opportunity, free of supervision overhearing his remark, then strongly comments,

"I remember when working for this company was fun!"

Such a statement is indicative of a salesperson passing through the transition from a first to a second generation selling style.

They have learned that their activities will no longer suffice in lieu of productivity.

They have experienced management's demand for sales to new classes of trade, new types of business or simply new prospects or new clients.

They have experienced management's demand for sales to new classes of trade, new types of business or simply new prospects or new clients.

They are pressured to sell the whole

When salespeople exclaim, "I remember when working here was fun," it indicates there is no longer any challenge in the job.

Second generation salespeople evolve to product oriented peddlers and are seldom productive long term.

product line and they must take action.

Again they respond,

"I remember when working here was fun," then continues "but if that's what they want me to do, I'll do it!"

Stalking back into their territory this transitional salesperson will call on the new prospects, they'll seek out different classes of trade, they'll even mention some of the other products. They'll go through the motions, they'll detail product after product, service after service, feature after feature, and then almost in a daring manner...perhaps over-simplified...they'll ask of the prospect, somewhat threateningly,

"Do you need any?"

These are the symptoms of a first generation COMMERCIAL VISITOR entering the second, just as disastrous, PEDDLER generation of selling skills.

The salesperson has become a *product-oriented* PEDDLER and he has become so because of pressure. Pressure is most often associated with the "top-down" phenomenon. The pressure that management exerts on subordinates to get them to change their skills. In this case such a

PROBLEM AREAS FOR SALESPEOPLE

IDENTIFYING THE REAL BUYING INFLUENCE IN A COMPANY
32%

determination is premature. Management can legislate more actual numbers of sales calls. Management can legislate the usage of certain sales tools. Management can even legislate work plans or hours on the job. Management pressure, however, will not mandate or effect an actual change in selling skills in this decade however.

In the case of such salespeople in the transition to second generation selling techniques pressure is evident but the pressure is "peer group pressure" and has little to do with management controls or management legislation.

A salesperson will be motivated to consider different selling skills only when pressure results from other salespeople who with the same products, same prices, same management and other department support are out-selling and out-producing the COMMERCIAL VISITOR by large margins.

This "peer group" pressure removes all the crutches the sales rep may have had and makes mandatory that he or she change to a more professional selling skill.

Management pressure seldom results in improved selling skills, short term productivity is the only benefit.

Peer group pressure however removes all the crutches for non-sales performance.

Again, the "I remember when working here was fun" factor is evident and the changing salesperson unfornunately becomes a product-oriented-peddler...price-oriented, product-oriented and with little conception of their customers real needs.

An episode of the popular television series of the late seventies "All in the Family" makes the point even clearer. The situation as presented talked about a father and son driving at excess speed down a freeway. There was a terrible accident, the father was killed and the son, still alive, was thrown from the car.

An ambulance was called and a physician alerted.

The son was rushed as fast as possible to the hospital. A doctor was on alert and as the physician began to operate the doctor quickly stepped back and exclaimed,

"I can't operate on him, he's my son!"

Think about it, what's the answer to the riddle?

How can it be?

The father was killed in the auto accident?

Simple...the physician, the doctor,

PROBLEM AREAS FOR SALESPEOPLE

SELLING PRICE INCREASES
28%

was the boy's mother!

The point suggests that even today some salesmen find it difficult to recognize peers in terms of women. In this case as hundreds of thousands of ladies enter the sales field, literally free of preconceived ideas as to how they should function, many will implement almost all of the basic selling skills some salesmen have discarded long ago. In this example the professional just happens to be female. Peer group pressure can and will result from a sales representative, male or female, young or old, who is simply using all of the basic fundamental skills mandatory to selling;

Planning skills, selling-tool usage skills, prospecting skills.

Third or fourth generation selling skills, analytical, needs-analysis skills.

The experienced, seasoned "comfort level" peer counterpart exposed to identical circumstances and skills may very well respond,

"I remember when working here was fun!"

The new salesperson, man or lady, has not as yet discovered that she or he can

A checklist of the basic, fundamental mandatory skills for selling success in your industry is a required tool today.

delete most of these mandatory requirements and still make a living as a "fair to adequate" sales rep. They plan, they organize, they 'problem solve,' they prospect. Their selling skills 'evolve' to more professional levels and their resultant productivity generates 'peer group pressure' on the entire sales team.

Peer group pressure creates PEDDLERS. Peddlers are individuals who mentally or physically carry the product into the customer and begin with a product "pitch."

Point by point, feature by feature, their competence in detailing each of their products is without question. If their products are transportable many have the trunk of their automobile loaded with samples or models. When one recognizes that the most productive professional sales representatives in the world *never* sell on the first sales call it makes the effectiveness of the PEDDLER who does, somewhat questionable.

The most productive salespeople worldwide rarely, if ever, sell on the initial sales call.

A professional third or fourth generation salesperson's initial activity is to discover the customer's needs, from the customer's point of view. Their objective

PROBLEM AREAS FOR SALESPEOPLE

COMMUNICATION WITH MANAGEMENT 28%

is to gain credibility. Their function is to conduct an in depth customer-needs-analysis. All mandatory activities which preclude any discussion of product or service.

Fifty percent of all people selling today are product oriented PEDDLERS who if in hearing their own sales call would note that most characteristic is the fact they, in almost every case, establish only a one-way communication with the client. The salesperson to prospect communication. There is very little dialogue. There is very little determination of the customer's needs from the customer's point of view.

In the 1950's and 60's it was quite common for recruiters of sales reps to seek out the legendary glib, six foot two, former quarterback, president of the student council, blue-eyed, blonde graduate. Today recruiters aren't so sure.

There is evidence to suggest that some characteristically introverted people can become professional, productive salespersons. It is suggested this is so because an introvert comes already equipped with *listening* skills and the

One half of all the individuals who sell, unfortunately, are product oriented peddlers.

"...some candidates for sales positions already come equipped with the most effective selling skill...the ability to listen."

most effective sales types have the listening ability in abundance.

PEDDLERS place their emphasis on their product and feel working for the company has ceased to be fun.

Third and fourth generation sales professionals cannot sell on the initial sales call because their goal, their objective is to first identify the customer's needs from the customer's point of view and then to satisfy those same needs profitably with tailored systems rather than isolated products or components.

THE
PROBLEM
SOLVER

This third generation sales professional is one of the newer breed of salespeople. They possess all the product knowledge of the peddler. They have the loyalty and commitment of the commercial visitor but those factors are their foundation or base not descriptive of their whole self.

Hannan, Cribbin and Heiser writing in their book CONSULTATIVE SELLING have detailed the how-to of this salesperson in depth. This well written book has been called the bible of third generation sales types and it is recommended reading.

Several other indicators also help formulate the identification of the PROBLEM-SOLVER sales type. First they have empathy in depth. The counselor salesperson is so desirous of being of sincere value to their clients that they are motivated to conduct a customer needs analysis with each new client and as well annually with all existing accounts. The counselor's needs analysis begins with a questioning exercise of the prospect, incorporating open-ended questions. This type of probing is a fundamental third generation selling techni-

Third generation salespeople have empathy in-depth. They are desirous of being of sincere value to the customer.

que. Open-ended questions cannot be answered "yes" or "no" and they facilitate the customer's response. It communicates interest and it creates an environment wherein the prospect freely communicates his needs.

The objective is to identify the customers needs from the customers point of view!

The objective is to identify the customer's needs from the *customer's point of view.*

A PEDDLER identifies needs in terms of his own products. The customers need equipment, textiles, a cleaning service, food stuffs, whatever the product may be. The PEDDLER does not have the capability of seeing beyond their own interests, their own products, their own objectives and their own needs.

The problem solver, however, identifies needs from the customer's point of view and will isolate safety, productivity, R.O.I., profit, decor, sanitation, etc. as the true customer needs, and therefore the "buying motive." They seek to solve real customer problems...to contribute, to deliver value, as well as product.

Professional salespeople seek to solve real customer problems.

Their empathy causes them to follow this "questioning exercise" with a *physical survey.* The hands-on, look-see of the client's operation often, as described later in the TEAM SELLING PSYCHOLOGY chapter, is in concert with others from the sales rep's firm.

Most uniquely this third generation sales type emphasizes solutions to problems, not products, but solutions and systems to solve their customers problems!

Characteristically following such an in-depth customer needs analysis the PROBLEM SOLVER still will not enter into a product presentation. Their professional response to clients most likely would be,

"I believe I understand your situation and needs...look, I'd like to discuss what I've learned with other members of our company's team and if we can come up with some solutions to help, may I get back to you?"

Research has shown the client will almost always enthusiastically respond,

"Yes, why, yes, of course."

The third generation PROBLEM-SOLVING type salesperson will exit at this point and will do so *almost universally without discussing their products.* If one should ever, as leaving, quickly turn to see their prospect's reaction they may very well witness a very startled expression. The prospect's thinking is,

"That sales rep didn't try to sell me anything. My God, I think he's interested in me!"

"Why that sales rep didn't try to sell me a thing...I sincerely believe he's interested in me and our problems."

What results is *credibility* and today that factor is mandatory in selling. The empathy ingredient in the counselor PROBLEM SOLVING salesperson was effectively described in an article published in the *Harvard Business Review* in the July/August issue of 1964 titled "What Makes A Good Salesman" and authored by David Mayer and Herbert M. Greenberg.

"Our basic theory is that a good salesperson must have at least two basic qualities: empathy and ego drive."

"Our basic theory is that a good salesman must have at least two basic qualities: empathy and ego drive.

Empathy, the important central ability to *feel* as the other fellow does in order to be able to sell him a product or service, must be possessed in large measure. Having empathy does not necessarily mean being sympathetic. One can know what the other fellow feels without agreeing with that feeling.

But a salesman simply cannot sell well

PROBLEM AREAS FOR SALESPEOPLE

CONFLICT BETWEEN WORK AND HOME SITUATION
23%

without the invaluable and irreplaceable ability to get a powerful feedback from his client through empathy.

A parallel might be drawn in this connection between the old anti-aircraft weapons and the new heat-attracted missiles. With the old type of ballistic weapon, the gunner would take aim at an airplane, correcting as best he could for windage and driftage, and then fire. If the shell missed by just a few inches because of a slight error in calculation or because the plane took evasive action, the miss might just as well have been by hundreds of yards for all the good it did.

This is the salesman with poor empathy. He aims at the target as best he can and proceeds along his sales track; but his target — the customer — fails to perform as predicted, the sale is missed.

On the other hand, the new missiles, if they are anywhere near the target, become attracted to the heat of the target's engine, and regardless of its evasive action, they finally home in and hit their mark.

This is the salesman with good empathy. He senses the reactions of the customer and is able to adjust to these reactions. He is not simply bound by a prepared sales track, but he functions in terms of the real interaction between himself and the customer.

Sensing what the customer is feeling, he is able to change pace, double back on his

Sensing what the customer is feeling a counselor sales type can adjust to home in on the target.

track, and make whatever creative modifications might be necessary to home in on the target and close the sale.

Need to Conquer

The second of the basic qualities absolutely needed by a good salesman is a particular kind of *ego drive* which makes him want and need to make the sale in a personal or ego way, not merely for the money to be gained. His feeling must be that he *has* to make the sale; the customer is there to help him fulfill his personal need. In effect, to the top salesman, the sale — the conquest — provides a powerful means of enhancing his ego. His self-picture improves dramatically by virtue of conquest, and diminishes with failure.

Because of the nature of all selling, the salesman will fail to sell more often than he will succeed. Thus, since failure tends to diminish his self-picture, his ego cannot be so weak that the poor self-picture continues for too long a time. Rather, the failure must act as a trigger — as a motivation toward greater efforts — which with success will bring the ego enhancement he seeks. A subtle balance must be found between (a) an ego partially weakened in precisely the right way to need a great deal of enhancement (the sale) and (b) an ego sufficiently strong to be motivated by failure but not to

The salesman's feeling must be that he has to make the sale!

PROBLEM AREAS FOR SALESPEOPLE

HANDLINGOBJECTIONS
18%

be shattered by it.

The salesman's empathy, coupled with his intense ego drive, enables him to home in on the target effectively and make the sale. He has the drive, the need to make the sale, and his empathy gives him the connecting tool with which to do it."

Additional references to describe the attitude of PROBLEM SOLVING and customer-oriented selling skills were hinted at in the publication "The Management Grid" and later "The Sales Grid" by Robert R. Blake and Jane Strygley Mouton, professors at the University of Texas and now management consultants.

(See Figure 1.1)

A salesperson's empathy, coupled with an intensive ego drive enables them to successfully close more sales.

GRID FOR SALES EXCELLENCE*

1,9 People Oriented	9,9 Problem Solving
I am the customer's friend. I understand him and respond to feelings and interests so he will like me.	My consultation informs me of customer needs. We work on a decision which yields expected benefits.

5,5   Sales Technique
My tried-and-true routine gets
a customer to buy.
It motivates him through a
blended "personality" and
product emphasis.

1,1 Take-It-Or-Leave-It	9,1 Push-The-Product
I place the product before the customer and it sells itself as and when it can.	I take charge of the customer...hard-sell them. Pile on all the pressure it takes to make a sale.

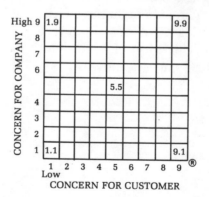

* **Note:**   The original concept for looking at the sales process on a grid network was developed by Robert R. Blake and Jane Srygley Mouton. Their work was published in a book originally titled *The Grid for Sales Excellence* and later reprinted under the title *Guideposts for Effective Salesmanship.*

Fig. 1.1

The "Sales Grid" suggests that a scale of 0 to 10 be used along one side of graph to rate "concern for the company" and that a similar scale be placed along the top of the grid to evaluate "concern for the customer." Each salesperson, every company, depending on the empathy for customer needs can be rated with a two-digit evaluation. Should the sales rep be possessed of internal motivation seeking only what is good for their company and themselves they would score a 10-0 on the grid. Maximum concern for the company and little concern for the customer. Such a sales rep most probably has first or second generation selling skills. If, however, the salesperson must continually have the lowest price to effect a sale, must always have the best deals or credit terms, must always have the widest range of style or colors...this 'give the customer whatever, no matter what he asks'...then he can be rated as a 0-10 on the marketing grid. Maximum sympathy for the customer and no concern for the company. Neither company will survive today. The "Sales Grid"

Only 8 out of every 100 salespeople evolve to third generation, consultative, selling skills.

publication correctly suggests that a 5.5 selling psychology results simply in survival and that a 9.9 sales psychology (ten, ten would be perfection) is the PROBLEM SOLVING selling skill of today.

A selling strategy that produces maximum benefit for the company while simultaneously delivering maximum value through the marketing of "systems" to the customer. One can only provide that value as a sales rep if they correctly perceive their role to be to *identify and then satisfy customer needs profitably.*

As apparent as these facts may be, only eight percent of all persons engaged in the selling function have evolved to this very proficient professional skill level.

Those who have, have a very remarkable competitive edge.

THE SUSTAINING RESOURCE

Only a miniscule one percent of all the world's salespeople have evolved and progressed to the fourth, most professional level of selling skills.

Due in part to the fact that many third and fourth level types are recruited for sales management positions with the hope of transferring their skills to others. Such a small share of the world's professionals with this ability creates an environment where they, instead of seeking out the customers, clients in fact, solicit *them*.

The SUSTAINING RESOURCE is a stature and image that progresses beyond the empathy of the PROBLEM SOLVER. The SUSTAINING RESOURCE level sales person must have PROBLEM SOLVER needs identification skills and produce a 9.9 service to company and customer yet they have a definite *expertise* that in itself has a monetary value to the customer.

Because *expertise* is most often a component of their systems and provided often cost free as part and parcel of the sale, this person, the SUSTAINING RESOURCE, is much in demand. He or she

Only 1% of the people who sell acquire an image and skill of 'sustaining resource.'

They know their customers business as well as they know their own.

The SUSTAINING RESOURCE type salesmans customers requests are for 'HELP' more than for product.

knows the customer's business as well as he knows his own. Their credibility is such and their expertise so complete that with regularity the sales rep receives an invitation to participate in the formulation of the prospect's goal setting, the client's five or ten year planning and forecasting activities.

This is not blue sky!

It's a function many salespeople engage in daily.

Their customer's requests are for 'help' more than for product.

The story is told that in the early years of computers a well known manufacturer's attempts to sell and to penetrate the computer sales market was unsuccessful. They took their in-house computer specialists, experts in their fields, and had them venture out to sell computers to the banking industry. It was only natural that when the company's computer specialist spoke with bankers he or she talked computers. Sales were less than they desired and the penetration of the market was far below their expectations. SUSTAINING RESOURCE level sales representation was needed. Shortly

PROBLEM AREAS FOR SALESPEOPLE

PROVIDING BETTER SERVICE
18%*

thereafter this computer manufacturer recruited and hired bankers. A basic but complete training program in product, in computer technology was given each new banking-background employee. These sales reps were then assigned functional territories rather than geographical areas. Territories based on classes of trade or types of business rather than geographical boundaries. They were bankers selling to bankers and when they called on bankers they talked *banking*. Computer sales then, it is said sky-rocketed. The banking industry began to perceive the computer company's representatives as knowing their business as well as they knew their own plus they seemed to have a certain *expertise* that offered the bank an ongoing, continuing, sustaining resource of business information which the bank could 'tap' as needed, when needed, where needed if they happened to be buyers of this manufacturer's computers. A sustaining resource selling skill level.

Factually, the salesperson has fourth generation, sustaining-resource type

*A decline from 48% in the three previous years.

You are a fourth generation salesperson when the customer perceives you to be an unpaid staff member in the customers employ.

selling skills at that point their prospects or clients perceive them to be an unpaid staff member in the customers employ. Such a skill, such an identity in the marketplace provides such sales types a form of invincibility in the eyes of the competitor.

There is a real danger in telling or suggesting to salespeople of many years *how to* sell. This book will not attempt to do so.

The salesperson must regularly "get-in-a-darkroom-with-themselves" and evaluate their own evolutionary process and honestly evaluate where it is they rest in terms of other selling personnel's "fair to adequate" capabilities.

Management, likewise, would be unwise to dictate how each salesperson should sell although it is appropriate that they set uncompromising minimum standards in terms of the mandatory skills of planning, prospecting, selling tool usage, administration, organization, etc. The professional sales rep, however, is challenged not entirely by management today. They are challenged by the daily asking of themselves the question,

"How will I do, in my territory, if it is the competitive salesperson who is doing these things?"

"How much will I produce if they are PROBLEM SOLVERS and I remain a COMMERCIAL VISITOR?"

"How effective will I be if I rest comfortably as a product-oriented PEDDLER and the competitor rep in this geographical area evolves to the SUSTAINING RESOURCE competency level?"

If the salesperson is honest and realistic with themselves they do not have to be told how to sell. . . they know what it takes and they are in fact in a constant evolutionary process to the fourth generation level. The Sustaining Resource type.

The three steps to this level of professionalism are clear indeed.

Step one is *exposure* to the skills, the systems, the techniques and the abilities of the professional. This book and the salesperson's company and its executive management have the accountability for providing that exposure to the concepts and techniques of third and fourth

How will I do in my territory if it is the competitive salesperson who does these things?

PROBLEM AREAS FOR SALESPEOPLE

MAKING TOO MANY CALLBACKS
16%

The accountability for exposing the sales team to professional selling skills is upper managements.

The accountability for training in terms of skills development is that of the line sales manager.

It is on the third step to professionalism where most salespeople falter...PRACTICE, of the necessary selling skills.

generation sales types. The format may be meetings, training programs, printed matter, personal development seminars, whatever. The accountability for exposing a company's sales team to the systems, however, is that of upper management.

The second step to professionalism is the equal responsibility of line, in-the-field supervision and the company's staff personnel if any. This step titled, "training," is the exercise that transforms information into skills.

It most often takes place "in-the-field," on-the-job with salespeople who have salesmanagers functioning as a coach. The ability to utilize and implement the learned information. The functioning of line management in a coaching posture.

The third and final step, however, is the step upon which most of the evolving salespeople fail. This step is called *practice*. The salesperson's first attempt at a customer needs analysis, the questioning exercise or the physical survey most probably will be less than desired. There has to be a high degree of "ego-drive" so as to self motivate the salesperson to try

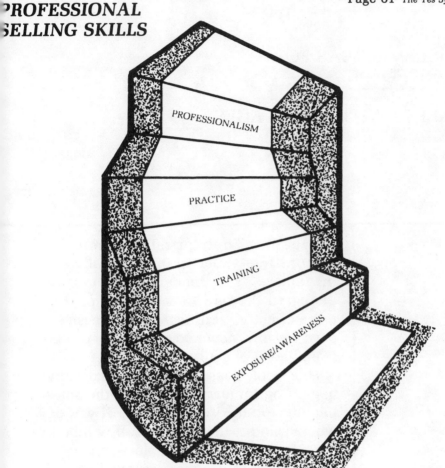

Step one: 'Exposure' to the concepts is the company's responsibility.

Step two: 'Training' (in skills) is the sales manager's accountability.

Step three: 'Practice' is the sales person's responsibility.

Step four: Third or fourth generation professional selling skills are the result.

Fig. 1.2

PROBLEM AREAS FOR SALESPEOPLE

DEALING WITH SHORTAGES
15%

Selling skills development should be evolutionary, not revolutionary.

Sales professionals understand there is only one way to develop new selling skills. . . to learn by doing.

it again. Their first attempt to demonstrate expertise may equally end in failure. The tendency then is to disregard the newer, more challenging, more effective abilities, and to cease the practice and never to achieve a professional level of selling skill.

This book does not even suggest that beginning tomorrow morning the salesperson stop talking "product." If you do, we guarantee, the salesperson will be in serious productivity trouble. Such an immediate departure from an existing selling style or technique is revolutionary not evolutionary. With any form of revolution. . .the unplanned, immediate, uncoordinated, overnight change, people get hurt and in this case the "people" are salespeople.

Once a representative becomes aware of a need to effect a transition from first and second generation skills to third or fourth generation techniques, for a person of average intelligence, we believe the transition period to be eighteen to twenty-four months.

People "learn by doing" and practice is the key ingredient to effect a positive change.

Earlier we suggested that novice salespersons lacking confidence or adequate skills historically call on small, less challenging, less demanding type accounts. The fact is true. When, however, the salesperson evolves to PROBLEM SOLVER or SUSTAINING RESOURCE skill levels they will be enjoying successes with the larger, higher-volume, more-sophisticated customers. At that point the desire to call on smaller accounts will cease. The motivation will be to sell only the major accounts. The day that transition takes place you will be faced with a far different set of circumstances. You will have salespeople who no longer call on smaller, less challenging, less demanding type accounts and that segment of the business will have to be sold by others.

There develops today in companies: different type sales areas, varied strata of territories. Commercial visitors improving or departing.

Product oriented peddlers with responsiblity for small, less sophisticated type accounts and third or

3rd and 4th generation salespeople generally lose the desire to call on small accounts.

Stratifying sales territories improves market penetration and increases productivity.

PROBLEM AREAS FOR SALESPEOPLE

SELLING TO GROUPS
12%

How many, if any, of your customers are calling asking for help?

fourth generation type salespeople, accountable for major type customers.

The evolutionary process PEDDLER skills and others have progressed to Problem Solving ability levels and subsequent territories.

There is again a definite method of ascertaining if you or your sales force are perceived by the market to be either PROBLEM SOLVERS or SUSTAINING RESOURCE level sales types.

Monitor a few days' telephone calls to office and salespeople. Determine how many are requesting certain products and as well determine how many, if any, of the customers are requesting *HELP!*

A company that receives no customer requests for expertise, for problem solving and for HELP has a sales force of COMMERCIAL VISITORS and PEDDLERS and they are in trouble!

Overall the objective today for both the salesperson and their company is to satisfy the requirement demanded so completely in illustration 1.3. This "notice" signage rests on the desk of former Mobil Oil Corporation executive, Robert Greenfield. Today an independent retailer in the Chicago market Mr. Greenfield requires his purveyors provide him plans and ideas rather than products...it should likewise be the objective of all professional salespeople.

NOTICE

If you want to sell your product to our company, be sure your product is accompanied by a plan, which will so help our business that we will be more anxious to buy than you are to sell.

D.W. Beveridge, Jr. and Associates

P O BOX 123   BARRINGTON   ILLINOIS   60010

MANAGEMENT AND MARKETING CONSULTANTS

Fig. 1.3

Can Eight Words Make a Better World?

Doctrines,
credos,
manifestos,
laws,
declarations,
codes of ethics.
Ever since
people
have been
able to communicate,
they have compiled
words to live by.
But the world
is still troubled.
Take these words:
honesty,
workmanship,
ambition,
faith,
education,
charity,
responsibility,
courage.
Chances are
four and a half
billion people
won't agree to
live their lives
by them.
But think how
much better
your life
would be if
just one person does.
You.

A message as published in the *Wall Street Journal*
by United Technologies Corporation, Hartford, Connecticut 06101

Fig. 1.4

TEAM SELLING PSYCHOLOGY II

PART II
TEAM SELLING PSYCHOLOGY

You may be sure that to be effective today as a salesperson you'll need the active support of many people...management, service departments, production, engineering, distribution...everyone. The "fighter pilot" selling strategy is no longer possible. That is the independent, on your own, dog-fight, dependent-on-singular-daring, risk, and bravado. It simply doesn't work today.

Instead today's successful salesperson has a self-image of an OR-CHESTRATOR.

Similar to the symphony conductor who can blend the best of string, percussion, wind and brass musicians...to generate harmony to produce a smooth, functioning sound, the salesperson of today has a similar job description. It is today's salesperson's responsibility, it is their accountability to orchestrate all the participants in their company and customer's environment so as to ensure we identify and satisfy the customers' needs profitably. That concept, that function today is the number one job priority of astute, professional salespersons.

"...to be effective as a sales person today you'll need the active support of many people."

"...the function of today's salesperson is to take on the role of 'orchestrator.'"

IT ISN'T THE INCOMPETENT SALESPEOPLE WHO
DESTROY AN ORGANIZATION, THE INCOMPETENT
NEVER GET IN A POSITION TO DESTROY IT. IT IS
THOSE WHO HAVE ACHIEVED SOMETHING AND
WANT TO REST UPON THEIR ACHIEVEMENTS
WHO ARE FOREVER CLOGGING THINGS UP.
—F.M. YOUNG

A signed order is not enough. It is only the first component of the sale.

Simply finding prospects to whom he/she can make presentations highlighting product features and benefits is in most cases the activities of only a "fair to adequate" salesperson. It's an elementary, amateurish level relative to today's selling techniques.

The professional salesperson is much, much more. The initial component in their "system of selling" is a TEAM SELLING PSYCHOLOGY.

They motivate, they sell, they encourage, they communicate with, they challenge, they orchestrate all members of their company's team; production, engineering, 'tech' service, service, management and as well all involved interested parties in their prospects organization. They orchestrate everyone!

A signed order is not enough, an obtained contract is only the first component in the sale...the professional salesperson *after* the buyer commitment, becomes an orchestrator of their company's resources to ensure the customer's needs are satisfied.

Typical of most companies is the

reverse. They have a "tumor," a business attitude "cancer" that must be removed. They suffer from the "Them Syndrome."

Characteristic are the responses marketing/management consultants receive when they begin their analysis in any one of many company departments. If one asks the production department where or what are the problems in the firm, the consultant is quickly referred to the service or administrative functions. Production perceives the company's problems to be elsewhere. When probing service or administrative department, again the consultant is advised to "look closely" at the sales department. If one talks to the salespeople, the listener's ears will be filled with the supposed asinine decisions of management.

If we can imagine a three-legged stool and title the seat area of the stool with the name of a company, then each leg independently with the name of a company department, then you can conceptualize the "them-syndrome." In verbage, in attitude and in actions each department tries to unscrew the

The cancer of most companies is the growing 'THEM SYNDROME' tumor.

In verbage, attitude and actions each department attempts to unscrew the other-guy's-leg.

Fig. 2.1

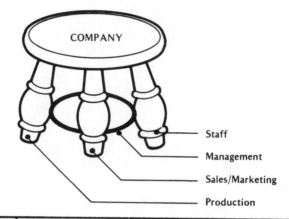

COMPANY

Staff

Management

Sales/Marketing

Production

other-guy's-leg. The tumor, the cancer is to sincerely believe it *is* the other guy and only the other guy. To believe it is the other department who needs improving and certainly not you or your own division.

Such an attitude on the part of a salesperson invites failure. He or she will not question if they are prospecting effectively; they will not see the absence of a work-plan, an itinerary, as the problem; they will shrug off criticism of verbal-only sales presentations as a problem when they know very well that sales presentations incorporating visual aids, selling tools, increase buyer retention of facts from 10% to 80% of what was discussed. They simply do not perceive that their skills, their attitude, their sales ability, may be part of the problem. It's much easier, simpler, to vocalize the shortcomings of service, of management, of production, whoever.

It has often been suggested that many salespeople subconsciously hope these supposed other department deficiencies are never ever corrected. You see, chances are *their* sales productivity

Selling tools increase buyer retention of facts from 10% to 80%.

would not increase in such a circumstance anyway and what would they then have available to be used for their "crutch" for the non-attainment of realistic sales goals? It's a thought.

A professional salesperson today is attuned to their role of orchestrator and they ensure the involvement of other company team members, of other departments, and of the customer, from the beginning to the closing of a sale.

There are other major differences between selling today and selling yesterday.

All professional salespeople, when selling, begin with a customer needs analysis *not* with a product presentation. Rarely will a professional ever sell or talk product on the initial sales call. The effort, the objective, is to uncover, to discover, true customer needs.

Described in HOW-TO detail in other chapters, this customer needs analysis has component parts in which a salesperson with a team selling psychology solicits participation by others in their firm.

In a manufacturing environment the salesperson's initial questioning may

A professional salesperson today is attuned to their role of orchestrator.

The objective is to uncover, to discover, true customer needs.

Customer needs are never for your product or service. The needs are always safety, economy, efficiency, convenience, R.O.I., decor, image, etc., but never for the product.

Two components of a needs analysis are the questioning exercise and the physical survey.

have uncovered needs for improved safety or increased productivity; in a restaurant situation a need for upgraded decor or more "store traffic;" in the analysis of a business, a need for better R.O.I (Return-on-Investment) or more profits may be uncovered.

Certainly the needs "from the customer's point of view" are endless. From the salesperson's point of view they are limited...limited to his products.

When a sales representative identifies their customers' needs from the customer's point of view, it presents selling opportunities that allow participation by other team members and other company departments to determine how to satisfy these customer-point-of-view "needs."

A skilled, professional sales-type will organize further analysis perhaps in the form of a "physical survey" of the business. This hands-on, empathetic, how-can-we-help activity is not simply a salesperson walking around the business with a pencil and paper. Five years ago, yes...but not today. The salesperson, might and should recruit a representative from their own production depart-

THE #1 JOB PRIORITY OF THE SKILLED, PRODUCTIVE SALESPERSON IS TO IDENTIFY AND THEN SATISFY THE CUSTOMERS NEEDS...PROFITABLY!

ment to join them in the "look-see" survey to identify safety or productivity improvements for the factory. They may solicit their company's management inputs for improved decor ideas for the eating, drinking and dining client. The salesperson continually inquires;

"Got any ideas?"

..."See any way we can help?"

Our professional may very well orchestrate involvement from their company's finance or administration departments to seek out solutions for the business needing R.O.I. improvement and profits-problem-solving.

Got any ideas? How can we help? Peers or staff should be encouraged to perceptually participate in the problem solving.

We are not suggesting that peers or staff join the field salesperson on most of their sales calls. It's not practical. We are suggesting, however, that within a progressive company today everyone...administration, staff, marketing, production, finance, engineering...everyone, does see as their number one job priority the responsibility to participate in the IDENTIFICATION and/or SATISFACTION OF THE CUSTOMER'S NEEDS...PROFITABLY.

Such a team selling psychology is a

"...identify then satisfy the customers needs...profitably."

constant, continuous activity.

Still greater, even more significant differences are evident.

Many professional sales-types actually incorporate a similar participative selling component when constructing a proposal. This selling tool or document today is far more than a superficial communication of product specifications and/or "grocery-list" pricing. The antiquated item by item listing of product or price that accompanies most quotes or bids is truly unimpressive in selling today.

To incorporate and communicate a team selling psychology and to secure a commitment from other company team participants, sales representatives have at times included a page in their proposals titled, "COMMITMENT CERTIFICATION." (See illustration). As a result of orchestrating other company personnel in the problem solving or selling function, either mentally or physically, the salesperson may ask their peer in production,

"Here's the quality level and delivery dates I'm offering the customer, can we

EXAMPLE: PROPOSAL COMMITMENT CERTIFICATION.

Unique to the proposals of our company is an emphasis on systems solutions to our client needs. The following signatures are warranty that these same systems have been reviewed by the involved parties and committments that the indicated departments will function so as to satisfy those same identified needs of the customer.

Charles W. Williams   8-15-81
Charles W. Williams, Account Manager   Date

Arnold B. Baker   8-16-81
Arnold B. Baker, Service Representative   Date

Thomas L. Paulie   8-17-81
Thomas L. Paulie, Production Manager   Date

Wilson Tomlinson   8-17-81
Wilson Tomlinson, Engineering   Date

T. J. Osborne   8-22-81
T. J. Osborne, General Manager   Date

Fig. 2.2

A COMPANY IS KNOWN BY THE PEOPLE IT EMPLOYS

Secure management and staff accountability with the executed COMMITMENT CERTIFICATION.

do it?"

With an affirmative response the salesperson turns to their "COMMITMENT CERTIFICATION" page of their proposal where they have a signature line with the production participant's name typed in below and states,

"Okay, I agree, please sign our certification so the customer sees this as not just a salesperson's promise but rather as a commitment from the company as a team."

At times you'll get a startled reaction, quickly followed by the production department representative's request to look more closely at the proposal. They may offer more ideas or suggestions to ensure the package 'works.' Having to sign one's name does much to generate a greater commitment to satisfying the customer's needs because it quickly makes your supporting departments more accountable.

Very quickly this production person becomes a part of the sales team.

This process is repeated with all involved departments and with management as well. It solicits participation, it

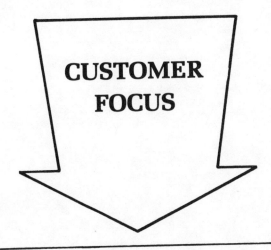

CUSTOMER FOCUS

mandates an emphasis on problem solving, it ensures the implementation of, and a commitment to, a team selling psychology. Factually a new "unique competitive advantage emerges," that does not require new technology, new products, or price concessions.

Importantly, in our view, no one, no department, in any company is free of responsibilities for participation in the identification and/or satisfaction of the customer's needs profitably. All have accountability to the customer. We recognize that a production line assembler, or a janitor, is well removed from actual customer contact. They do, however, still participate in the team selling psychology. The company janitor should be asked to list his primary job priority. If his response is to "sweep the floor," the company has a problem.

Ask the salesperson what they perceive to be their own number one job priority. If they respond, "to sell this stuff," the company has a problem.

Talk to the company's chief executive officer, ask him/her for their job priority. If the response is, "profit, bottom

Everyone in the company has or should have accountability to the customer.

line," well, there's trouble brewing.

In the above, each of the company's personnel voiced a true job function, activity, or goal. The number one job priority without a doubt, at all levels, however, must be to IDENTIFY AND/OR SATISFY THE CUSTOMER'S NEEDS PROFITABLY...and that includes the salesperson.

When the janitor recognizes that his efficient, effective control of the company's dust and dirt in actuality sets the firm's first "standard" for product quality and that he in fact is a real participant, a real component of the team's desire to satisfy true customer needs...the plant will be much cleaner.

The example is not far-fetched. Job enrichment author and researcher Douglas McGregor's* studies on "Significant Work" proves the application and potential of such an involvement.

Today those firms who can generate a team selling psychology have a competitive edge, and such advantages over competition result from the efforts of professional sales-types who see their

Those firms who can generate a team selling psychology have a competitive edge.

*"The Human Side of Enterprise"...by Douglas McGregor

function as much more than glib, verbal, humorous communicators. They function effectively as orchestrators, coordinating, stimulating, organizing, involving, orchestrating the company's varied resources to the point the delivered product or service is actually a system of needs satisfying, problem solving, value for a satisfied client.

The delivered product is actually a system of needs satisfying value for the customer.

Don't Be Afraid To Fail

You've failed
many times,
although you may not
remember.
You fell down
the first time
you tried to walk.
You almost drowned
the first time
you tried to
swim, didn't you?
Did you hit the
ball the first time
you swung a bat?
Heavy hitters,
the ones who hit the
most home runs,
also strike
out a lot.
R. H. Macy
failed seven
times before his
store in New York
caught on.
English novelist
John Creasey got
753 rejection slips
before he published
564 books.
Babe Ruth struck out
1,330 times,
but he also hit
714 home runs.
Don't worry about
failure.
Worry about the
chances you miss
when you don't
even try.

Fig. 2.3   A message as published in the *Wall Street Journal*
by United Technologies Corporation, Hartford, Connecticut 06101

A UNIQUE COMPETITIVE EDGE III

PART III
A UNIQUE
COMPETITIVE
EDGE

Whatever it may be, this "unique competitive advantage" is vital to the success of a salesperson or company. On rare occasions such unique advantages have created environments where companies and industries were lulled to sleep believing their product or market share prevented competitive inroads. General Motors Corporation's dominance for years of the automotive market brought them to a "comfort level" where they saw their competition as Ford and Chrysler and to a corporate attitude of believing they could dictate the customers' needs rather than satisfy the customer's *changing* needs.

In 1979 and 1980 the Japanese auto manufacturers, more empathetic to those changing needs, developed a "competitive advantage" and secured large shares of the car market. Fuel economy received the most press coverage but the Japanese product also featured higher quality, craftsmanship in the assembly, practical and futuristic options and a solid, functional product.

Another example of a lack of empathy for customers' changing needs was "Ma

Companies and salespeople reach comfort levels believing they can dictate the customers needs. They can't!

Bell." For years almost totally void of competition their marketing philosophy rivaled very closely Henry Ford's rumored strategy of yesteryear, "you can have any color car you want as long as it's black." At AT&T you could have any color phone you wanted as long as it was black. In the nineteen eighties, the nation's giant telephone companies were in a toe-to-toe battle to maintain their market share. In the 1960's and 1970's colored phones were introduced. . .reluctantly. In 1980 they introduced Mickey Mouse phones, executive phones plus a variety of broadened services and products to satisfy changing customer needs. The activity was a "revolutionary" process, however, of unplanned, crisis, emergency type marketing as opposed to the more desirous "evolutionary" process of planned, constant change.

No company, no salesperson can survive, produce, profit without a unique competitive edge.

No company, no salesperson can survive, produce, profit without a unique competitive edge. The problem or the opportunity is to ensure that as a salesperson you conceptually, factually recognize what that advantage or edge

YOU WILL NEVER EVER AGAIN, LONG TERM, HAVE A COMPETITIVE ADVANTAGE IN PRODUCT OR PRICE!
—Don Beveridge

most often is. . . and it will seldom, *long term* be either product or price.

In this regard most salespeople are "carriers." Selling in the field, a prospect responding to a request to buy might counter with,

"Hey, the competitor's price is five percent less."

Our carrier, the salesperson, pivots, returns to management expounding excitedly,

"I sold him, but our price is too high. What-d-ya want to do?"

They have carried the message to their company that they no longer have an edge. Ridiculously some firms return their representative to the battle with a lowered price. Within days or weeks there develops another crisis. The competitor now has a new color, a new style, is offering "bakers-dozens" or has attached a premium. The "carrier" again returns,

"I need a new color, a new style, a new deal, a newer product, etc."

Unfortunately, in their thinking the unique competitive advantages they request are dispensed by management, by

It is only in the very rarest of circumstances that the competitive advantage is in product or price.

In situations where such a wonder product or exceptional value does exist, there is a lessened need for field salespeople.

the company and have nothing or little at all to do with them.

Should a sales representative perceive their role, their skill, to be only that of carrying learned information back from their prospects to management for the company's renewal of a competitive edge they will not survive in selling as a career. It is only in the very rarest of circumstances...in quasi-monopolies... that a unique competitive advantage will ever continue in product or price, long term.

The telephone industry as well as General Motors had such an advantage, for a time; but that has changed and developed into a very competitive environment. The salesperson who waits in their territory for the new wonder product, for the unique function, for a new style or color, or for a lowered price or deal is immature. In most cases the product, price or deal will never come. The AT&T monopoly was rare. The General Motors dominance unique.

In situations where such a wonder product or exceptional value does result there is a lessened need for field

EMPATHY, EXPERTISE AND PROBLEM SOLVING SKILLED SALESPEOPLE ARE TODAY'S UNIQUE COMPETITIVE ADVANTAGES
—Don Beveridge

salespeople. The product sells itself. Rarely will your unique competitive advantage materialize in product or price. Reduce your price and the competitor will quickly match the number. Build a new product feature and in days the characteristic is copied in a similar product...and those are facts!

Factually the objective is to generate an edge, an advantage in the activities and skills of the salesperson. The salesperson, themselves, are the unique edge. Their empathy, their expertise, their problem solving orientation. When the professional salesperson is compared to their peers who are described as having abilities that are only "fair to adequate" they clearly stand alone.

The real objective is to develop an edge, an advantage in the activities and skills of the salesperson.

Today only forty percent of what successful firms bring their customers is their product or service. Sixty percent of what is delivered are the support-programs, the other system components that make the product/service perform to the customer's satisfaction.

Only 40% of what your customer buys is the product. 60% of the buying decision is based on the other components in your system.

You may quickly determine the components in your own system by compiling an in-depth list of answers to the question, "What do we do for the customer beyond the product?" With few items listed you are at a selling disadvantage.

A professional salesperson doesn't sell the product or service...their edge, their unique competitive advantage is the fact that they sell "the system." The integrated components of product, services, programs, analysis, financing, engineering, implementation, whatever, into a *tailored system* to satisfy the customers' needs.

Professional salespeople confess that similar services or products can be obtained from many of the competitors...at times at a lesser price.

They'll continue, however, that buyers must be suspect of firms or salespeople (including themselves) who quickly suggest products and/or services without knowing the customer's true needs and of salespersons who ask the customer to pick what he wants rather than professionally telling him what he needs. In the former selling skill, if your product or service doesn't satisfy his needs, do you ask the customer to pick again? Not

Professional sales types do not ask the customer to pick what he wants. They tell them what they need.

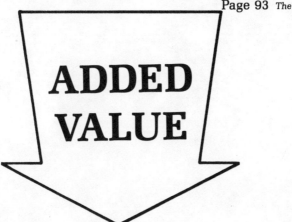

ADDED VALUE

hardly. The professional sales representative *tells* their customers what they need and retain the accountability for it meeting those needs.

Often a professional sales representative today will describe their selling technique of needs analysis, questioning exercises, physical surveys, as the initial component...the sales component...as a phase in the system.

They may detail their firm's "team selling psychology" and department-by-department commitment to customer satisfaction as still another component in the system.

Many detail a "planned value evaluation" phase where a future date is determined to return to the client...prior to problems with the existing systems surfacing, as a component in the system. A date where on a pre-planned basis another complete customer needs analysis is performed to identify changing needs and to ensure continuing value...as a component in the system.

That's selling today. Selling professionally today.

Sell the *system* not the product or service.

Emphasize the system as your unique competitive advantage, play down the product or service as having a uniqueness. Sell the "management" competency. Sell the biographical sketch of the "service-rep" who will handle the account. Sell the "testimonials" of others who benefit from doing business with you. (See Figure 6.3)

Sell the system.

Amplify the salesperson's abilities, your skills, your tailoring, your empathy, your expertise, your problem solving orientation, your SYSTEMS!

Maintaining that edge, it is understood additionally, requires the company and its management to also have responsibilities...to make marketing decisions which satisfy customers' needs as well as company needs.

Sell the system, not the product.

SELLING
THE
SYSTEM

The sales representative still has concurrent accountability, however, for establishing their firm's competitive edge in the marketplace. They remain as the "center piece" in the establishment of such an image.

Consistently, regularly professional salespeople ask themselves,

"How do my customers see me?"

If the answer quickly comes back... as a *product*, they're in trouble selling today.

Sales personnel whose identity is relative to their product are vulnerable to changing product features in the competitors' line. They are vulnerable to price variations and they are never perceived by the prospect as being able to provide help and expertise beyond the features and benefits of their own products.

Paramount to this phenomenon taking place is the "goals attitude" of the today salesperson. How it is, he or she conceptually understands what the commitment to the quantified and qualified goals must be. An interesting comparison is to ask of salespeople which of

Professional salespeople consistently ask themselves, "How does the customer see me?"

Goals are...
Guidelines?
Targets?
Something the company
would like you to hit?
...or mandatory?

the four following definitions most adequately describes a "goal." How they sincerely, honestly understand and feel about their sales objective. This analysis requires the salesperson to select just *one* of the definitions which follow although all may seem similar. Take the time to make your own analysis...

Read, think about and analyze each of the following:

1. A sales goal is a guideline.
2. A sales goal is mandatory.
3. A sales goal is a target.
4. A sales goal is something the company would like me to achieve.

Think about it...now select your definition of a sales objective.

Which do *you* believe is most applicable?

Research established that well over half of all salespeople describe their sales objective as a guideline or target. A situation quite frankly where there exists no crisis to perform, and in today's markets a description no professional salesperson would select.

About thirty-seven percent of the sales representatives respond that the goal is something the management or the company, "would like them to hit." In this case the salesperson subconsciously feels the objectives are the company's goals, "not my goals." Rarely are they achieved. They view the objective as not being *their* goal . . . it's a company objective.

Only nine percent* of all salespeople perceive their sales goal to be *mandatory* and therein lies the problem of ensuring a unique competitive advantage.

Only 9% of all salespeople perceive the sales goal to be mandatory.

We suggest the next time we as salespeople travel by aircraft, prior to boarding the plane, we ask of the pilot how *he* feels about his goal of returning the aircraft safely to the originating city.

Is it a guideline?

Is it mandatory?

Is it a target?

Or is it something the airline company would like him to do?

If the pilot fails to immediately respond "mandatory, it's mandatory we land safely," . . . well, get off that airplane.

With a mandatory goals attitude, to land the aircraft safely in the intended

*The balance have no goals and function under the philosophy of, "I do the best I can."

"I HOPE WE ARE OVER OUR BELIEF THAT IF YOU DEFINE A PROBLEM YOU DON'T HAVE TO DO ANY WORK."
—Peter Drucker

Professionals in any business sincerely believe they must find a way to make it happen.

city, as the minimum acceptable standard of performance, the pilot takes actions in spite of weather, in spite of maintenance deficiencies, in spite of crisis, to land safely on target.

Resultantly an unbelievable percentage of commercial aircraft do land safely relative to the huge number of air miles logged. A professional, competent, productive salesperson has a similar understanding of their goals.

They must find a way to make it happen!

In spite of price, in spite of production or management deficiencies, in spite of competition they must find a way to attain the objective. It's the sales rep's responsibility. It's the professional's accountability.

Most salespeople demand that production meet their targeted delivery or quantity commitments and they demand so without question. Most insist that administration and/or management follow through on commitments they have made to the customer. The salesperson certainly, without exception, would become irate if the person accountable for getting their salary or commission checks to them on time didn't consider *their* goal to be mandatory. Why then is it any different for sales reps?

Factually, it isn't!

The professional salesperson understands that every year, every month, every day there exists logical, honest, realistic, rational reasons as to why they will not achieve their target. The professional sales representative casts these crutches aside as does the professional pilot, bad weather, maintenance problems, whatever. The professional is in themselves "the unique competitive edge." Their competency, their empathy, their expertise, their ability to tailor systems to satisfy identified customer needs far outdistance any momentary price or product advantage of the competition.

Their system of selling as a sustaining resource to their clientele creates a logical rather than emotional relationship with the prospect.

Their proposals are customer needs oriented, not price-oriented 'spec' sheets.

Importantly, the professional salesperson doesn't ask the customer what he wants...*they tell him what he needs*. They, without doubt are the edge, the unique competitive advantage.

The professional salesperson's philosophy can be summed up with this simple statement:

IF IT IS TO BE IT IS UP TO ME!

Get Out Of That Rut

Oscar Wilde said,
"Consistency is
the last refuge of
the unimaginative."
So stop getting up
at 6:05.
Get up at 5:06.
Walk a mile at dawn.
Find a new way
to drive to work.
Switch chores with
your spouse
next Saturday.
Buy a wok.
Study wildflowers.
Stay up alone all night.
Read to the blind.
Start counting
brown-eyed blondes
or blonds.
Subscribe to an
out-of-town paper.
Canoe at midnight.
Don't write to your
congressman,
take a whole scout
troop to see him.
Learn to speak
Italian.
Teach some kid
the thing you do best.
Listen to two hours of
uninterrupted Mozart.
Take up aerobic dancing.
Leap out of that rut.
Savor life.
Remember, we only
pass this way once.

A message as published in the *Wall Street Journal*
by United Technologies Corporation, Hartford, Connecticut 06101

Fig. 3.1

STANDARDS OF PROFESSIONAL SALESPEOPLE IV

STANDARDS OF PROFESSIONAL SALESPEOPLE

An opportunity exists to observe, with a minimum investment of time, the professional level and future potential of any sales team and organization. The technique allows for a "visual" check of almost one hundred percent of any sales force and is without fail in its suggested conclusions.

It is proposed that one arrive at a sales meeting room approximately thirty minutes prior to the announced commencement of any sales meeting. Now, as each salesperson enters, note how many of the reps arrive with pen and paper. Look to determine what percentage of the salespeople actually attend ready to listen, to learn, to participate and to *take notes*. If the large majority of the meeting participants are attending without such required information recording material...a simple yellow note pad...that organization is at a "comfort level!"

What they are visually communicating is the fact that they are as good as they are ever going to be. They have a mental set of;

"What else could I possibly learn. I'm

If the salesmen show up for a sales meeting without note paper...they're at a comfort level and that organization is in trouble.

as good as I need to be."

There are three other 'verbal type' indicators that can be observed when a salesperson has ceased evolving. You will hear them, in all sales groups, in every company...and they clearly predict future selling productivity problems.

Such sales people are often heard to say,

"I wonder what they'd do if I ever left this territory?"

The answer by the way is usually, "better."

They'll next vocalize when confronted with a need for improved skills,

"I do the best I can."

That always suggests the salesperson is at the peak of his or her capability, and finally,

The salesperson in trouble follows months later with,

"We're different."

It's their attempt to shake off the peer group pressure by discounting the effectiveness of sales personnel in other companies or industries.

These salespeople are informing the

company's management that the productivity "monkey" is on the company's back and it isn't the salesperson who requires changing. These salespeople are at a "comfort level" and highly resistive to improve, to change or to meet other professional standards of salesmanship.

One of the standards of a professional salesperson is that they are in a constant learning posture. They are continuous in their quest for improved skills or techniques. They are almost laborious in their quest for more information. They are not at a state of static skills or declining standards, or a "comfort level." The professional knows, he or she has more to learn.

Professional sales-people are in a constant learning posture.

Such a salesperson wouldn't consider attending a sales meeting without pen and note paper.

In each of the primary selling skills there exists wide, measurable differences in each of the four generations of sales types.

Percent

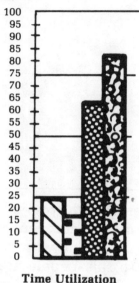

**Percentage
level of
effectiveness**

Time Utilization

Fig. 4.01

GENERATIONS OF SELLING SKILLS EFFECTIVENESS COMPARISON CHART

 1st Generation
Commercial Visitor

2nd Generation
Peddler

 3rd Generation
Counselor

 4th Generation
Sustaining Resource

Time Utilization
Not in terms of hours worked but rather the skilled, effective utilization of the hours spent on-the-job. Planning, organization as well as the ability to "trim-the-fat" from the actual sales call.

Percent

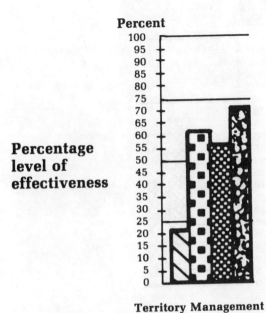

Percentage level of effectiveness

Territory Management   **Fig. 4.02**

GENERATIONS OF SELLING SKILLS EFFECTIVENESS COMPARISON CHART

 1st Generation Commercial Visitor

 2nd Generation Peddler

 3rd Generation Counselor

 4th Generation Sustaining Resource

Territory Management

The ability to control the territory as opposed to the territory taking control of the salesperson. Programmed coverage, control of crisis, reduction of repetitive customer contacts to accomplish the same task, the targeting of accounts and specific objectives for the calls.

Percent

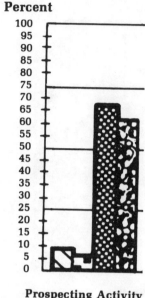

**Percentage
level of
effectiveness**

Prospecting Activity　　　　**Fig. 4.03**

GENERATIONS OF SELLING SKILLS EFFECTIVENESS COMPARISON CHART

 1st Generation
Commercial Visitor

 2nd Generation
Peddler

 3rd Generation
Counselor

 4th Generation
Sustaining Resource

Prospecting Activities

The ability to 'self-generate' prospects, to insure an evolution of clients and to designate an actual percentage of the salesperson's time for calling on wholly new accounts. The practice of by plan, by design both adding and consciously dropping existing accounts annually.

Percent

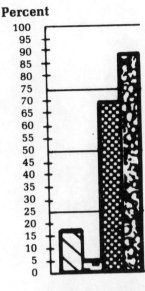

Percentage level of effectiveness

Selling Tool Usage   Fig. 4.04

GENERATIONS OF SELLING SKILLS EFFECTIVENESS COMPARISON CHART

 1st Generation
Commercial Visitor

 2nd Generation
Peddler

 3rd Generation
Counselor

 4th Generation
Sustaining Resource

Selling Tool Usage

Films, brochures, specification sheets, proposals, etc., all incorporated as an integral part of the salesperson's presentation.

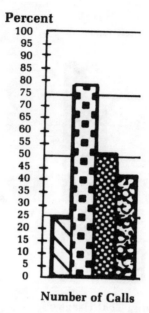

Percent

**Percentage
level of
effectiveness**

Number of Calls

Fig. 4.05

GENERATIONS OF SELLING SKILLS EFFECTIVENESS COMPARISON CHART

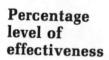 1st Generation
Commercial Visitor

 2nd Generation
Peddler

 3rd Generation
Counselor

 4th Generation
Sustaining Resource

Number of Calls

The physical number of calls made by the salesperson in terms of the percentage of total calls reported by all salespeople in a particular company, division or branch for the period.

Percent

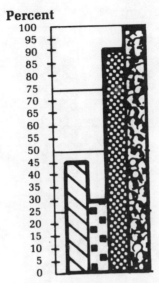

**Percentage
level of
effectiveness**

Image of Professionalism   **Fig. 4.06**

GENERATIONS OF SELLING SKILLS EFFECTIVENESS COMPARISON CHART

 1st Generation
Commercial Visitor

 2nd Generation
Peddler

 3rd Generation
Counselor

 4th Generation
Sustaining Resource

Image of Professionalism

How the salesperson was perceived in terms of his or her 'professionalism' by the customers the sales representative was selling. Their image, their identity and in terms of the customers willingness to have the salesperson return.

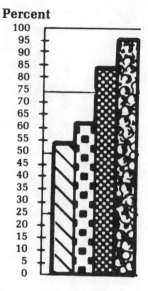

Percent

**Percentage
level of
effectiveness**

Goal Attainment   **Fig. 4.07**

GENERATIONS OF SELLING SKILLS EFFECTIVENESS COMPARISON CHART

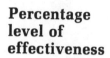 1st Generation
Commercial Visitor

 2nd Generation
Peddler

 3rd Generation
Counselor

 4th Generation
Sustaining Resource

Goal Attainment
The percentage of times the salesperson exceeded realistic, attainable but stretch sales goals.

Percent

**Percentage
level of
effectiveness**

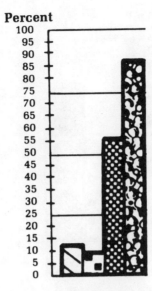

Product Mix

Fig. 4.08

GENERATIONS OF SELLING SKILLS EFFECTIVENESS COMPARISON CHART

 1st Generation
Commercial Visitor

 2nd Generation
Peddler

 3rd Generation
Counselor

 4th Generation
Sustaining Resource

Product Mix
The percentage of the product line
sold by the salesperson.

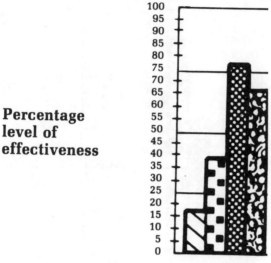

Percent

**Percentage
level of
effectiveness**

Customer Mix　　　　　　**Fig. 4.09**

GENERATIONS OF SELLING SKILLS EFFECTIVENESS COMPARISON CHART

 1st Generation
Commercial Visitor

 2nd Generation
Peddler

 3rd Generation
Counselor

 4th Generation
Sustaining Resource

Customer Mix

The percentage of the potential 'classes-of-trade' sold or called on by the salesperson who were viable prospects for their products or services.

GENERATIONS OF SELLING SKILLS EFFECTIVENESS COMPARISON CHART

(Data based on in-the-field observations and analysis, 1970 through 1981 by D. W. Beveridge, Jr. & Associates, Barrington, Illinois of 547 salespersons in multiple industries.)

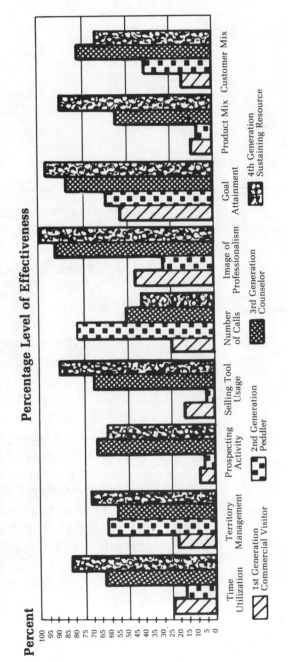

Percentage Level of Effectiveness

Percent

100 95 90 85 80 75 70 65 60 55 50 45 40 35 30 25 20 15 10 5 0

Time Utilization · Territory Management · Prospecting Activity · Selling Tool Usage · Number of Calls · Image of Professionalism · Goal Attainment · Product Mix · Customer Mix

1st Generation Commercial Visitor
2nd Generation Peddler
3rd Generation Counselor
4th Generation Sustaining Resource

Fig. 4.0

Prospecting Systems:

Other known *standards are even more* elementary.

The standard of functioning in a constant *"prospecting"* posture is also characteristic of the professional salesperson. Earlier we warned of "whittling the territory down to the good ole boys." This situation takes place when there exists no infusion of wholly new accounts to the present customer/client list. It's a disastrous circumstance in that as new customers develop and evolve they must go to one of the competitors. The lack of time is most often offered by salespeople as to why they don't prospect. Recognize that all professional selling personnel also face time management problems. Not having enough time to solicit or call on wholly new prospects is the most offered crutch for not prospecting on a continuous basis. Professionals conceptually understand that a sales territory must be in an evolutionary process as well. Today's best accounts tomorrow may be a phased out company. Tomorrow's breadwinner may well be an emerging

What percentage of your time are you calling on 'wholly-new' accounts?

Customer lists should be in an evolutionary state.

industry as was the plastics or computer business just a few years ago.

The need for constant prospecting is evident and a professional by design, by plan, adds and as well drops accounts annually. Those clients who are diminishing in terms of the return on invested selling time must be replaced with new prospects of emerging potential and their demise is a coordinated, pre-planned, programmed, by design, professional sales rep's decision. It's not necessary to lose these customers completely and their decreasing purchases volume totally. These reduced-purchases-accounts can be put into a phone or mail territory in which the salesperson handles their needs more quickly, without a physical field visit or with reduced contacts.

Specifically, ask yourself, "What percentage of your time are you now calling on wholly new accounts?"

Can you answer?

Those salespeople who are characteristically the achievers, the producers, the sales leaders in a company will, without hesitation or emotion res-

Productive salespeople by plan, by design, drop accounts annually so that there is time to add new business.

pond,
"10%" - "15%" - "50%". . . or some other percentage.

The percentage they voice is unimportant in that the amount varies by the needs of any particular territory. The important fact is that they have a known, committed, mandatory, measurable goal for the efficient usage of their selling time. . . and a committed portion of that plan for prospecting and calling on wholly new accounts.

The finding of new prospects is a mandatory selling standard.

The finding of new prospects, is a mandatory selling standard and each industry has a multitude of systems for doing so.

Most effective in all prospecting systems is the *referral* system.

The word referral itself often suggests that such leads be generated from an existing customer group who are satisfied with the value received in the product or service.

Not necessarily so!

Its meaning and the technique used are broadened greatly in terms of their use by a third or fourth generation sales type. Recall how somewhat poorly cer-

GOOD MEN WITHOUT A SOUND PLAN ARE
INEFFECTIVE
—Woody Hayes

tain marketers of insurance have been
schooled to solicit referrals and prospects. At the conclusion of an insurance presentation, and whether the
policy has been sold or not, the limited-
skilled insurance rep almost by rote, inquires:

"Who else do you know who needs insurance?"

In many cases the buyer is actually re-
pulsed by this request to list family or
friends upon whom the representative
can call. It is a technique for obtaining
qualified leads but requires a PEDDLER
level salesperson to carry it off. In most
cases you'll find that type of request of-
fensive to the solicited client because the
unprofessional sales rep requests the
referral from *his point of view.*

His needs are paramount.

He requires names of people to whom
he can sell.

He requests the client *help him* rather
than vice versa.

Referrals are, however, a
professional's prospecting tool, only the
manner in which they are solicited dif-
fers greatly with professional sales

*Referrals are a
professional's
prospecting tool.*

types.

Third and fourth generation sales types recognize that indifferent to the fact they have or have not successfully consummated this particular sale, without fail, they do request referrals prior to the interview's termination. The difference, the professional edge, rests in the fact that the referrals are requested *from the customer's point of view* rather than from the salesperson's needs point of view.

Recall the PROBLEM SOLVER or SUSTAINING RESOURCE level salesperson as they initiate the system of selling with a customer needs analysis.

This professional becomes privy to this client's needs, to the customer's objectives, to the prospect's problems or goals. The sales professional solicits a referral utilizing the identified existing customer's needs as his or her basis for doing so.

If the identified need was in the area of "safety" our professional would inquire,

"Are other operations faced with safety needs?"

The client inevitably, simply to prove

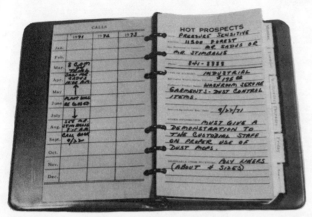

he is not unique or alone in his problem, will most often respond,

"Why, yes!"

The salesperson then matter of factly asks,

"Who?"

The salesperson is not naive enough to believe the client will follow with,

"Tell them I suggested you call . . . use my name."

That would be a very rare circumstance.

Factually the sales professional seeks in their referrals only two points. The name of the prospect and then, his or her real need. If the existing customer's identified need was "improved decor" the rep would ask,

"Are other establishments upgrading their decor image and appearance?"

Then follows with,

"Who?"

"Are other businesses in today's economy faced with R.O.I. difficulties?"

Again, "Who?"

A continuous prospecting posture and the constant request for referrals are a fundamental standard in one's selling skills.

The professional additionally has developed a physical prospecting system which is functional and with him or her "in the territory."

To be totally effective and as shown in the illustration 1) a prospecting system is most usable when it can be carried into the field. Systems back at the office or at home do not meet today's needs. 2) The system should have preprinted reminders...a checklist...of information needed about the prospect and most often available at the time of the referral if we remember to ask. 3) It should additionally have the capability of recording the "call history" and the activity which has taken place each time to ensure a progression to the sale. 4) The system finally should contain a group of dividers *not* alphabetically but rather dividers for the days and as well the months. Prospects are not filed alphabetically, prospects are filed by "contact dates or periods so that the entire list of future customers is in some phase of a contact plan. When a lead or prospect is uncovered and the informa-

EXAMPLE: PROSPECT BOOK

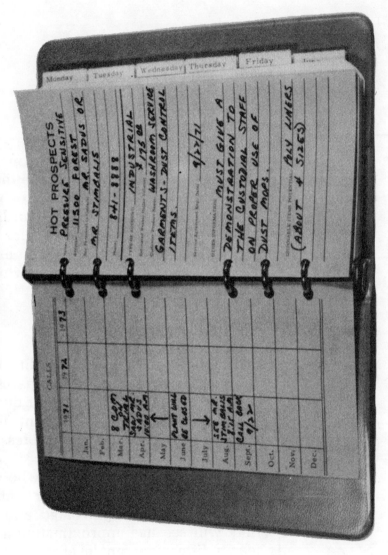

Fig. 4.1

tion recorded, the salesperson then decides whether they will make the call next week, or in a future month and the prospect's sheet is filed accordingly, simply, behind that particular tab, organized, ready for recall and/or review when there is no one on which to call.

Preplanned Activities

Although only one in eight of all salespeople consistently prepares an itinerary, a weekly, monthly, or quarterly work plan, this component is yet another standard of the professional sales type.

A field sales representative who waits until the day of his or her calls to organize where they will go and who they will see has approximately a thirteen to fifteen percent level of efficiency. They factually lose too much face-to-face sales time in that process.

If he or she is the type who appears regularly for phoned-in leads then it is their prospecting system that is not intact.

PROSPECTING SOURCES

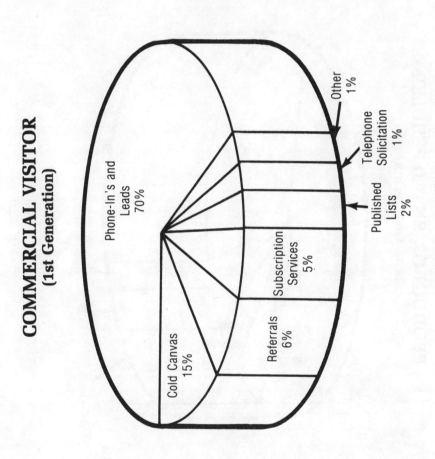

COMMERCIAL VISITOR
(1st Generation)

Phone-In's and Leads 70%

Cold Canvas 15%

Referrals 6%

Subscription Services 5%

Published Lists 2%

Telephone Solicitation 1%

Other 1%

Fig. 4.2

PROSPECTING SOURCES

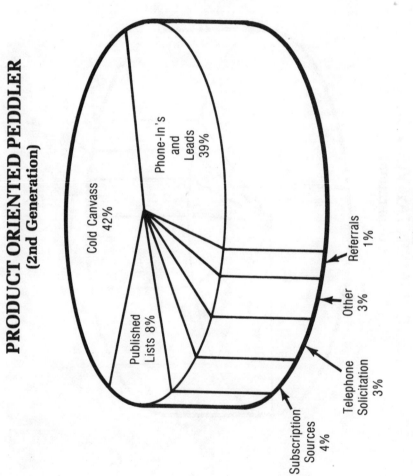

PRODUCT ORIENTED PEDDLER
(2nd Generation)

Cold Canvass 42%

Phone-In's and Leads 39%

Published Lists 8%

Subscription Sources 4%

Telephone Solicitation 3%

Other 3%

Referrals 1%

Fig. 4.3

PROSPECTING SOURCES

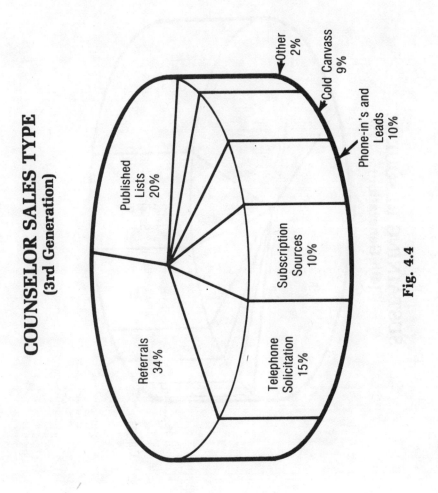

COUNSELOR SALES TYPE
(3rd Generation)

Referrals 34%

Published Lists 20%

Telephone Solicitation 15%

Subscription Sources 10%

Other 2%

Cold Canvass 9%

Phone-in's and Leads 10%

Fig. 4.4

PROSPECTING SOURCES

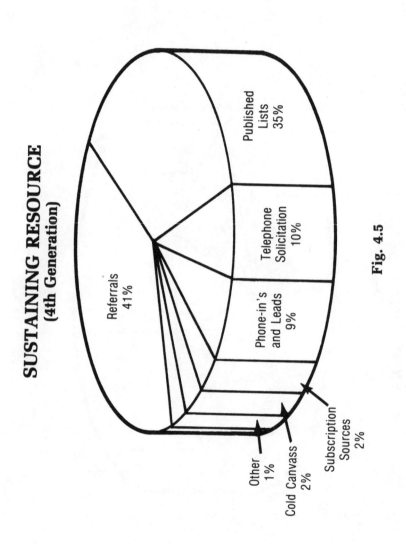

SUSTAINING RESOURCE
(4th Generation)

Published Lists 35%

Telephone Solicitation 10%

Phone-in's and Leads 9%

Referrals 41%

Other 1%

Cold Canvass 2%

Subscription Sources 2%

Fig. 4.5

Mistakenly many salespeople perceive the itinerary to be a company management tool. A system to police if they are working. Call reports still used by some companies (but in almost every case proven to be almost valueless) are a management tool that can be more closely related to such a supervisory policing activity. Call reports universally almost always only produce champion call report "maker-outers." Salespeople in such an environment consciously inquire of sales managers:

"Tell me what you want on the call report and you'll get it."

Few are totally factual, many are fictitious and only some have value.

More importantly call reports are *after the fact*. Work plans, itineraries are *before the fact* and provide data and information upon which the sales rep can act.

Specifically an itinerary does not meet work plan standards if it simply is a listing of geographical areas. An effective work-plan-type itinerary lists for each day the *name* of the prospect or company and as well the *objective* of the

Mistakenly many salespeople perceive the itinerary to be a company management policing tool.

Call reports universally almost always only produce champion call report maker-outers.

Call reports are after-the-fact, work plans, itineraries are before-the-fact.

call. That's important!

The criteria available to judge the validity of an objective of the call is that it must be:

1. Specific
2. Attainable
3. Measurable
4. Stretch

Isn't it important that your company for survival have a broadened product-mix which ensures the marketing of the entire product line? Of course it is. Isn't it vital that a company enjoy a good customer-mix so it is not dependent or vulnerable to one industry or company? Of course it is.

A good 'call-mix' is mandatory by the sales team.

Then just as mandatory is a good 'call-mix' by the sales team which ensures that there exist sales calls in all phases of development.

Objectives listed may be cold canvas; customer needs analysis; physical survey; proposal delivery and close.

The objective of the call may be a planned value evaluation; a system implementation; a lead inquiry; etc.

The professional sales rep can weekly or monthly hold such a document, their itinerary and work plan, at arms length and compare it to their known *profile*. Let me explain.

Skilled salespersons at least on a quarterly basis view their sales to date and determine from the past quarter's work plans, itineraries what are the average number of calls daily during that period which resulted in the gained sales volume; they determine what were the number of proposals they delivered? What is their selling success and close ratio? (i.e., number of proposals delivered versus number of sales made.) These are factual pieces of information about their own techniques that resulted in a certain sales volume for the just passed quarter.

How many suspects had to be cold canvassed to secure a prospect with which a customer needs analysis could be completed? What percentage of their time was spent soliciting wholly new accounts?

All these facts and more are evident from the evaluation of the past work plans. When one compares his or her current itinerary, this period's plan,

Work plans are not simple geographical listings. Rather they list the name of the account and the objective of the call.

The workplan is a professional salesperson's standard tool.

with the known factors of the most recent period, *the known profile* emerges; and he or she also knows specifically the dollar sales volume such effort produced...well he or she can simply adjust their upcoming itinerary in those areas of need to reflect increased sales productivity.

The itinerary is a professional salesperson's standard tool. Management may desire same to be submitted weekly but its real value is to the sales rep themselves. It's the *barometer* of future productivity.

EXAMPLE: WORK PLAN/ITINERARY

Name CHARLES W. WILLIAMS

PRE-PLANNED ACTIVITIES

Week Beginning August 16, 1981

Gross Sales Goals: $140,000

Actual Year-to-Date: $86,617

	Monday	Tuesday	Wednesday	Thursday	Friday
	Account & Objective	Account & Objective	Account & Objective	Account & Objective	Account & Objective
Sales Presentations	I.K MART - OGDEN (present proposal) WHITE HEN, INC. (Installation) INTERLAKE (suspect) HOLIDAY VALLEY (suspect) NINO'S (present proposal)	So. Side Electric (Customer Needs Analysis) Ted's Fine Foods (Planned Value Evaluation) LANE FENCING (suspect) O'BRIEN RADIO (suspect)	MORNING TO HANDLE WEEK'S EMERGENCY'S MAIL OUT NEW MODEL BROCHURE TO "A" SUSPECTS BANTER PRESS (Customer Needs Analysis)	ABC METALS (Inventory for Reorder) Franklin Stoves (Sell-Close!) DARWIN'S SPORTING GOODS (Advertisement response-lead) BARRINGTON INC. (SELL-CLOSE!)	TURNER FABRIC (Show new model - upgrade acc't.) BASIC SYSTEMS (collection of monies!) Sales Meeting
Other Activities			CHAMBER of COMMERCE DINNER		Half day sales meeting at training center

Fig. 4.6

**EFFECTIVENESS
USING/NOT USING
SALES TOOLS**

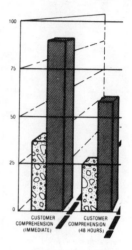

VERBAL ONLY
PRESENTATIONS

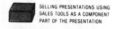

SELLING PRESENTATIONS USING
SALES TOOLS AS A COMPONENT
PART OF THE PRESENTATION

CUSTOMER
COMPREHENSION
(IMMEDIATE)

CUSTOMER
COMPREHENSION
(48 HOURS)

Selling Tool Usage

Still another standard of third and fourth generation selling skills is the consistent use of selling tools.

Wholly oral sales presentations miss the mark badly.

Wholly oral sales presentations and those that are all "talk" miss the mark badly. Even so, most salespeople fail to employ the available brochures, films, demonstration units and other selling tools available to them.

A manager of an oil company sales force in St. Louis called a sales meeting and as each of his sales reps arrived he directed them not into a hotel meeting room but rather to the rear parking lot of the motel. There he had the salespeople assemble their vehicles into a circle similar to the defenses of the western covered wagons under Indian attack. With a portable bull horn this sales manager asked the group to remove all sales material not in a condition they should be to be shown to a prospect. Next he had each remove any material they hadn't used in the past one hundred and twenty days. Finally prior to supplying each salesperson with an organized,

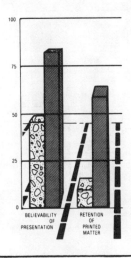

**EFFECTIVENESS
USING/NOT USING
SALES TOOLS**

 VERBAL ONLY
PRESENTATIONS

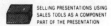 SELLING PRESENTATIONS USING
SALES TOOLS AS A COMPONENT
PART OF THE PRESENTATION

complete, fresh supply of selling tools he asked in general for any of the company's many existing brochures. One of his salespeople anxious for approval and recognition quickly offered one. The sales manager holding the brochure and taking two steps backward asked the salesperson,

"Tell me, what does this brochure specifically discuss?"

The salesperson gave a general response suggesting the brochure reviewed the product pictured graphically on the cover. The sales manager countered,

"I'm aware of the product described, but exactly *what* does it say inside the brochure?"

The startled salesperson was stumped and couldn't answer.

He fell silent.

Interestingly this embarrassed sales representative is not unusual. Factually only three of every ten salespersons have ever read their own brochures. They are not aware of what they say specifically and resultantly hardly ever use them as selling tools.

Factually only three of every ten salespeople have ever read their own brochures.

**EFFECTIVENESS
USING/NOT USING
SALES TOOLS**

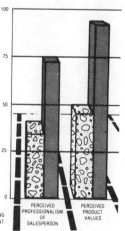

 VERBAL ONLY PRESENTATIONS

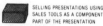 SELLING PRESENTATIONS USING SALES TOOLS AS A COMPONENT PART OF THE PRESENTATION

Use a yellow felt marker to overline those sentences which are pertinent to the identified customers needs.

A professional's technique is to know and understand each tool in depth. After determining a customer's need a skilled salesperson will use a yellow felt marker to overline those sentences or those paragraphs in applicable product brochures so that when he or she returns to make their presentation the selling tools have been *tailored* to that particular customer's *identified needs*.

Selling tools, whether brochures or films are also most often utilized incorrectly by most salespeople. Hand a client a brochure without relating his or her needs to same or show a prospect a film about your product or service in the initial sales call and most yawn or lose interest shortly after the title.

The reason?

Salespeople incorrectly utilize these tools as "shotgun," opening, interest-creating items.

They are not!

Selling tools are 'closing-the-sale' documents.

Selling tools are "closing-the-sale" documents. They are tailored with yellow felt marker to show pertinence to a particular customer's need.

Films are introduced in the close and

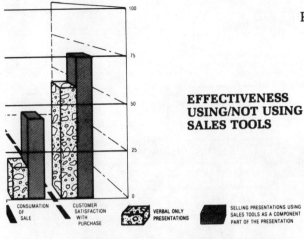

EFFECTIVENESS USING/NOT USING SALES TOOLS

CONSUMATION OF SALE

CUSTOMER SATISFACTION WITH PURCHASE

VERBAL ONLY PRESENTATIONS

SELLING PRESENTATIONS USING SALES TOOLS AS A COMPONENT PART OF THE PRESENTATION

the customer is alerted to watch for certain frames, certain sections or particular components of the audio-visual presentation because it will illustrate solutions to his specific problems. The sales tools insure 80% comprehension of the offered information; they allow the showing of the entire product line without carrying in tons of product samples; they professionalize the sales presentation and they are a professional's 'closing' selling tool.

ANALYSIS OF SELLING EFFECTIVENESS USING/NOT USING SALES TOOLS

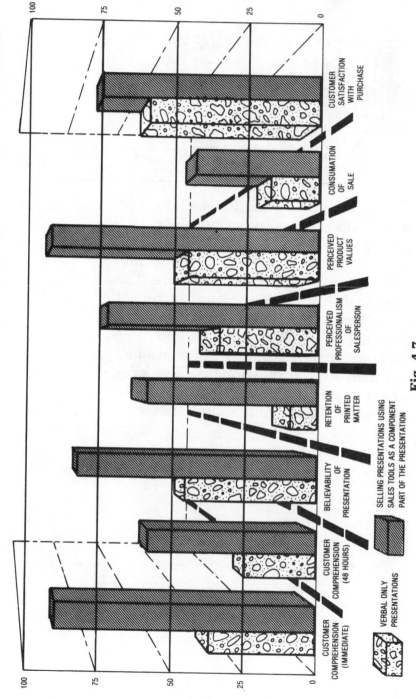

Fig. 4.7

Proposals

Selling tools today also incorporate the delivered proposal itself.

Almost antiquated is the product-oriented specification listing and the grocery-list pricing (item lists with the unit price following). Most commonly titled a 'quote' or 'quotation' this product-oriented, price-emphasizing, antiquated tool places the emphasis, as do PEDDLERS, on product and price.

The product and price-oriented, specification dominated proposal is antiquated.

Quite to the contrary today's proposals place heavy emphasis on the customer's needs and solutions to meet those needs. They contain a "critical path" which develops the format and scheduling for implementing the needs-satisfying systems and almost incidentally, finally, in retrospect, the "investment."

Today's proposals place heavy emphasis on the customers needs and solutions to his problems.

It's an emerging standard of professional selling skills and today's proposal, utilized as a selling tool, has these important factors:

The Carrier:

The proposal's "carrier" or cover letter *never*, under any circumstances, indicates suggested products or asking price. In fact the proposal is very seldom posted or mailed. It is almost always hand-delivered so that it can be utilized as a presentation piece. Additionally the proposal carrier (or cover letter) should contain a "tailored paragraph" which communicates both the range of what is offered as well as the fact the proposal has been tailored to the customer's unique needs. The opening paragraph might read:

Dear Mr. Smith:

The *programs, systems, service* and *products* described in this proposal have been tailored to the unique needs of your firm.

Immediately the buyer perceives "added-value" and begins to evaluate his or her desired investment to cover more than mere product. Additionally, he begins to feel secure that these "programs" were *tailored* to fit his needs.

Also contained in the cover letter is the expiration paragraph. Proposals are not offered to clients for time immemorial. They are not presented to be decided upon at the prospect's leisure.

Added value, tailored programs and expiration dates are key components.

TODAYS PROPOSALS ARE NOT PRICE AND SPECIFICATION ORIENTED. THEY ARE CUSTOMERS NEEDS AND PROBLEM SOLVING ORIENTED.

The carrier should contain a final paragraph which states,

"as described the proposal is available to ABC Steel through October 22, 1981."

The objective is to bring the prospect to a point of decision in spite of the fact the decision might be negative. Even with a "no" reply at least the salesperson recognizes he or she must again begin to sell. If the cover letter has no expiration deadline when the sales rep calls on the buyer and asks relative to a decision the response most frequently is,

"We're still looking at it."

In such a case the sales rep is deadlocked. They can't sell and they can't push. They simply must wait which makes them very vulnerable.

The objective is to bring the client to a point of decision... even if the decision is NO!

Commitment Certification:

As described earlier the carrier or cover letter is followed by the COMMITMENT CERTIFICATION page. The authenticating signatures of each of the selling company's varied department's personnel who either participated in the survey or will participate in delivering the promised customer benefits. This team selling commitment (not product warranty) is a dynamic component to a proposal and functions as still another unique competitive advantage of the professional salesperson.

The Actual Proposal:

The proposal itself follows and this document is physically most often typed double-spaced, has wide margins and has titled sections. The objective is to ensure the proposal is easy to read and allows areas in which the buyer can make notes. Buyer convenience is the objective. Each of the titled sections are as follows and each in turn has a definite role in the sale.

The objective is to ensure the proposal is easy (convenient) to read.

1. **Customer Needs Analysis...**
factually only a description of the selling company's survey. The objective is to detail in depth who looked, where they looked and when they looked, i.e.,

"On January tenth and eleventh Howard Brown and Diane Smith of Acme Services surveyed the facilities of ABC Steel in Cleveland, Ohio. An

PROPOSALS ARE RARELY IF EVER MAILED. THEY ARE HAND DELIVERED AND USED BY PROFESSIONAL SALESPEOPLE AS SELLING TOOLS.

analysis of work flow, productivity, safety factors and quality of product were the objective. Assembly, distribution and production were a few of many departments surveyed."

(Note, no products, no problems, no prices are discussed. Only the firm's survey is detailed.)

At this point in the presentation and using the proposal as a selling tool, after reviewing how it is the salesperson surveyed and determined the needs, the seller asks of the buyer,

"Is there any other place we should have looked?"

This technique of a professional selling skill is called the "yes-syndrome." The question gains commitment from the buyer. If his response is,

"Why, no, the survey seems complete." He has in reality said, "Yes, your survey is adequate."

He has bought that phase of your package and you can proceed to the next titled section.

If his response is,

"You should have met with research and development" . . .

The "yes-syndrome" is the professional salespersons closing skill;
Is there anyplace else we should have looked?

Diplomatically but as quickly as you can close your proposal and scurry over to R & D as fast as your legs will carry you. It's an indication of a poor job in the "questioning-exercise" phase of the needs analysis. Under no circumstances proceed to the next titled section unless he agrees or buys the validity of the survey.

Additionally, following the description of the survey, the professional proposal has a phase wherein lies the chronological list of the names and titles of every person in the prospective client's company who was contacted, interviewed or surveyed.

Is there anyone else we should have talked with?

This laborious listing adds *credibility* to the proposal suggesting that what follows are not just the beliefs of the selling firm but also that of the prospect's personnel.

Again, the "yes syndrome" is applied by the salesperson's inquiry,

Is there anyhing else you'll require?

"Is there anyone else we should have talked with?"

When your client says no, he has in fact responded affirmatively to your proposal to this point. He again is say-

MONIES LISTED IN A PROPOSAL TODAY ARE NOT
DETAILED AS COST OR PRICE. 'INVESTMENT' IS
THE WORD WHICH IS USED SUGGESTING THERE
WILL BE A RETURN.

ing, "Yes, I agree, please proceed."
2. The second titled section of the proposal should be "IDENTIFIED
NEEDS." This professional ingredient
in the proposal lists customer needs,
very importantly, from the *client's
point of view*. Here again, *no products,
no programs, no prices* are discussed.
Needs from the customer's point of
view are phrased,

"There seems to be a loss of prestige
and status to Armco Steel created by
the stained carpeting in the reception
foyer."

From the customer's point of view is
the terminology "a loss of prestige and
status to Armco Steel" versus a need
written as,

"Armco Steel requires new
carpeting in its reception areas."

Another example might be,

"There is a confirmed loss of productivity in Armco's production
facilities resulting in reduced efficiency and profitability created by equipment which cannot meet industry
standards."

Such a statement is far more

Don't you agree?

MARKET SYSTEMS

palatable to the prospect than,

"Armco needs presses and milling machines."

Here again following the discussion of each of these needs described from the customer's point of view the "yes syndrome" is applied. In this case the salesperson's question to the prospect is,

"Don't you agree?"

If the answer is 'yes' you have earned the right to proceed. If the answer is 'no,' go no further...you've lost credibility and maybe the sale. The salesperson's response to a negative answer in this section is simply,

"I'm sorry...I may have been using a different standard in my analysis. Let's you and I go together to the factory...to the foyer...to wherever we have suggested a need, and reappraise the 'need'...I believe you might then concur with my findings."

3. **Problem Solving** is the third titled section and although it is here the features and benefits of the products recommended are detailed, they are offered only as components in a

ONE STEP TO ENSURE YOUR PROSPECT ACTUALLY READS YOUR PROPOSAL IS TO USE THE WORDS FOR NUMBERS RATHER THAN NUMERALS. THEY'LL NOT STAND OUT WHICH REDUCES THE MOTIVATION TO READ THE NARRATIVE.

"system." The professional proposal does not only emphasize products. It is not an in-depth specification or pricing sheet. This phase of the proposal describes in-depth the entire problem solving package (systems) proposed to meet the identified needs, including most of those things you do for the customer beyond the product.

The "service" component, the "training of personnel" component, the "engineering" component.

The "follow-through" component, the "management of the systems" component, and as well the "product" component.

A total system is the real product. The "System" which satisfies the customer's needs with the "product" as only one of the offered components is the technique and the actual "product" of the professional.

Again we sell this phase by following the discussion asking (the 'yes' syndrome),

"Don't you agree?"

If the answer is 'yes'...he's buying so continue.

Incorporate in your proposal what it is you do for the customer beyond the product.

4. Following should be **Graphics**. The drawings, the brochures, the printed matter, the product literature, that have been "tailored" to the identified customer's needs.

   The product specifications and other features. Blueprints, and if applicable floor plans.

Printed materials add to the credibility of the proposal.

   Printed documents in a proposal serve as a form of testimonial. They add to the credibility, in that, separate from a verbal discussion and also independent of the typed page, buyers tend to believe that if it's printed...it's most probably true. These again are the brochures with yellow felt marker overlines. These are the documented 'plans,' these are the existing customer tesimonials if any.

   The yes syndrome is used again, we ask,

   "Is there additional documentation you might require?"...When he says

   "No, not that I can see," he has again said 'yes' to your graphics.

5. Long a management tool in the production environment and today an

assumed consent selling tool in sales, the proposal's next phase is the **Critical Path**. A series of dates, activities, and responsibilities, this listing begins with the first buyer/seller interview and continues through all of the assumed activities that the salesperson expects to take place. Activities such as "initial interview"; customer needs analysis; proposal presentation; letter of intent; contract execution; order placement; systems installation; etc.

Each activity is preceded with the intended date it will happen and followed with the initials of the responsible party (note illustration).

When the salesperson "sells" with this section he or she simply assumes consent and offers,

"We're looking at a project completion date of November 22nd."

The inference is that the dates are open for discussion, for approval, and that the purchase itself is assumed to have been already made.

6. What's missing from the document?

Most will suggest price or cost.

EXAMPLE: CRITICAL PATH PROPOSAL COMPONENT

Recommendations critical path:

Date	Activity	Responsibility
Feb. 2, 81	Initial interview	C.W.W. (salesman)
Feb. 21, 81	Second interview	C.W.W.
Mar. 14, 81	Survey & needs analysis	C.W.W.
Apr. 5, 81	Proposal presentation/ recommendations	C.W.W.
May 15, 81	Contract executed	H.L.B. (customer)
June 1, 81	Financing arranged	H.L.B.
June 2, 81	Products ordered	C.W.W.
July 10, 81	Prototype evaluation	H.L.B.
July 15, 81	Systems approved	H.L.B.
July 15, 81	Fifty percent deposit	H.L.B.
Aug. 1, 81	Site preparation	H.L.B.
Aug. 10, 81	Introductory meeting for customer personnel	H.L.B./C.W.W.
Aug. 15, 81	Systems installation	A.B.B. (service rep.)
Aug. 20, 81	Training classes/operations	A.B.B.
Aug. 21, 81	Training classes/adm.	C.W.W.
Sept. 1, 81	Systems operational	H.L.B./C.W.W./A.B.B.
Dec. 1, 81	Changing needs evaluation	C.W.W.
Sept. 1, 82	Planned value evaluation	C.W.W./A.B.B.

Fig. 4.8

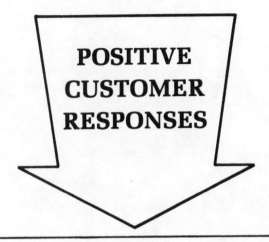

POSITIVE CUSTOMER RESPONSES

Not so!

In this final section the underlined title is recommended to be **Investment**. The word investment subconsciously suggests a *return*. Even so, it is proposed that a "grocery list" type pricing still *not* be used. The buyer will run his finger down that type of list until he finds something, no matter how small, that you are priced high on and a confrontation will ensue.

This final proposal component titled "INVESTMENT" should read:

"The programs, systems services and products as described and available through (expiration date of proposal) require an investment of approximately one hundred thousand dollars."

It is recognized that buyers want specific prices and definite costs. The professional salesperson however, has selling skills that allow them to delay providing those specific amounts until they have earned a verbal commitment to the package.

Price the system, the package, and

should a line-by-line, item-by-item listing be mandatory, indicate to the client that you of course will provide same at time of contract. The salesperson's comment might be:

"At this point we need to determine if the needs have been identified correctly; have we developed systems to meet those needs; is the time schedule applicable; and is there approximately this much value in our system?"

If you have incorporated the 'yes syndrome' selling skill to this point the buyer's response must be yes. He's been agreeing with each section or you wouldn't have gotten to this point in the sale.

There is also justification for using the word 'approximately' in this investment phase. The objective is to draw out from the buyer the competitor's offer or price prior to you being specific. If you list the exact amount, a buyer might respond:

"Oh, I can buy it from competitor X at 6% less."

Such a situation puts the profes-

sional salesperson in a disadvan-
tageous position. Should he or she
lower his or her price 6%, the salesperson loses credibility and the buyer
tries to get them even lower. If,
however, the salesperson has incorporated the verbage 'approximately,'
they are in a position to respond to the
brand X offer:

"I'm sure Mr. Buyer, when we
detail the package, item by item and
cost each we will be in the same investment area...maybe even
lower."

The competitor's lower price is
handled. The buyer feels confident he
is getting a 'good deal' and a sale
results.

Proposals of this type do require
professionalism, it does require a third
or fourth generation selling style and
it additionally requires physical labor.
It requires work!

Salespeople often question if such a
document is really necessary. To obtain an answer the salesperson simply
asks of themselves,

"How will I do in my territory if it's

the competitive sales rep who delivers this type proposal?"

The answer generally motivates us to deliver the same.

SALES LEVERAGING

(Notes: Illustration No. 4.90)

A summary of the information presented would suggest that prior to client or prospect contact...a neutral buying posture...is evident.

Leveraging a positive | buying decision or the feared 'NO'...negative buying decision | is influenced as much or more by the selling skills of the sales representative as it is by the quality of the product or service. The following two pages detail graphically the two alternatives.

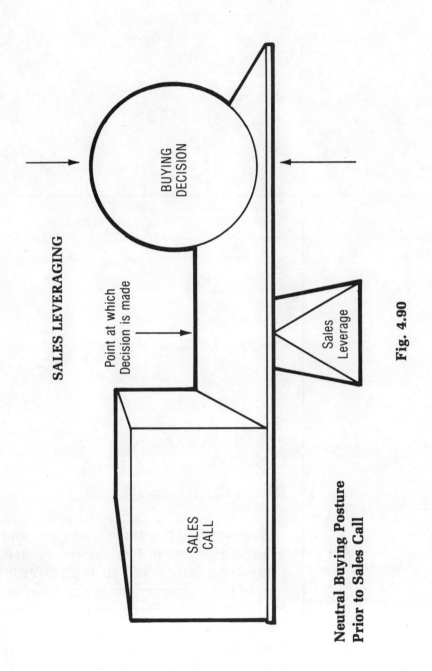

SALES LEVERAGING

BUYING DECISION

Point at which Decision is made

SALES CALL

Sales Leverage

Fig. 4.90

Neutral Buying Posture Prior to Sales Call

SALES LEVERAGING
(Negative)

(Notes: Illustration No. 4.91)

As described the 1st or 2nd generation salespeople are not customer focused. Little time is devoted to the identification of the customers needs so resultantly the greatest effort is spent in closing efforts such as price or deals. No matter how skilled the closing technique may be it is leveraged so poorly that the weakest customer objection is sufficient to generate a negative response to the proposal.

SALES LEVERAGING

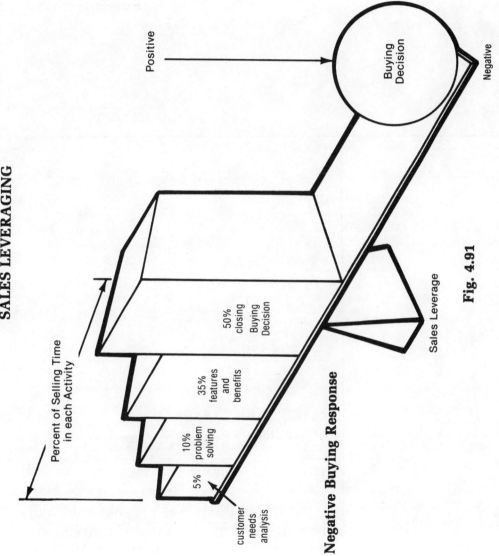

Fig. 4.91

SALES LEVERAGING
(Positive)

(Notes: Illustration No. 4.92)

Positive customer responses are leveraged by professional Counselor or Sustaining Resource sales types. They orient their client contact so much in the customer focus posture that closing the sale is almost taken for granted. It's not that easy we know, but the results are heavily weighed to favor the salesperson.

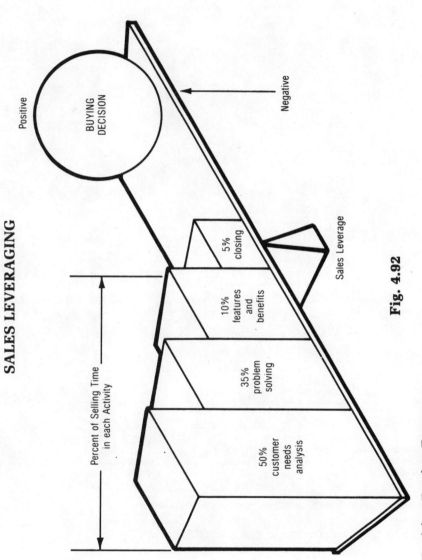

SALES LEVERAGING

Positive

BUYING DECISION

Negative

5% closing

10% features and benefits

35% problem solving

50% customer needs analysis

Percent of Selling Time in each Activity

Sales Leverage

Fig. 4.92

Positive Buying Response

It's What You Do– Not When You Do It

Ted Williams, at age 42,
slammed a home run
in his last official
time at bat.
Mickey Mantle, age 20,
hit 23 home runs
his first full year
in the major leagues.
Golda Meir was 71 when
she became Prime Minister
of Israel.
William Pitt II was 24
when he became
Prime Minister of
Great Britain.
George Bernard Shaw was 94
when one of his plays
was first produced.
Mozart was just seven
when his first composition
was published.
Now, how about this?
Benjamin Franklin
was a newspaper columnist
at 16,
and a framer of The United
States Constitution
when he was 81.
You're never too young
or too old
if you've got talent.
Let's recognize
that age has little to do
with ability.

A message as published in the *Wall Street Journal*
by United Technologies Corporation, Hartford, Connecticut 06101

THE CATALYST V

PART V
THE CATALYST

Perhaps no other criteria is as important as "HOW YOU SEE YOUR MANAGER" in determining if a sales rep will make the transition from first and second generation selling skills to third and fourth skill levels.

How do you see your manager? Your answer could determine your future success.

In most cases sales representatives have a choice of four images as to how they perceive the role of their leader.

Should that identity in the eyes of the sales personnel be any except the fourth managment image it has been the author's experience that the salesperson will probably not develop to the professional third or fourth generation skill level.

The Non-Manager

In primarily heavy commission-oriented selling environments the salesperson trends to a higher degree of independence. They see themselves as almost an independent businessperson even though they are actually an employee of their company. These salespeople typically voice their lack of a need for sales management and are highly resistive of in-the-field visitations

Whenever you're in an environment where there are no disciplines for non-performance, you always have declining standards.

by supervision.

Such salespeople see their boss as a NON-MANAGER. A manager whose only purpose it would seem is to process the salesperson's orders, to approve their deals, to function as the liaison between their territory and production...a NON-MANAGER.

In such a case there does not exist a manager/subordinate work relationship where there are *disciplines for non-performance.*

In all circumstances where salespeople function in such an environment you will witness declining standards in the sales team. Itineraries and work plans will have been discarded. Prospecting systems will no longer be in use. Selling tools and other components of the selling presentation will have been long deleted.

When there are no disciplines for nonperformance; when there is no continuing reaffirmation of selling standards; when the sales manager is seen as a non-manager and he or she functions in such a way, the selling team deteriorates in their abilities and both salespeople and manager are in trouble. Limited success

LEADERS HAVE TWO IMPORTANT CHARACTERISTICS; FIRST, THEY ARE GOING SOMEWHERE; SECOND, THEY ARE ABLE TO PERSUADE OTHER PEOPLE TO GO WITH THEM.

will be the constant companion of both salespeople and sales manager in such a case.

Frankly, supervisors cannot offer "challenge" in the job as non-managers. It is discipline that makes a challenge real. Should a salesperson function in an unchallenging environment, should they not be disciplined for sub-standard performance and achievement...their skills, their goal attainment and standards will continue to fall.

We often ask of sales managers,
"Have you had any turnover of people in your organization"
Some will tell us of resignations, still others will proudly respond that they have had no such turnover. Our response is to ask if the fact they have not had any management generated turnover bothers them? If the answer is no, we are quick to respond... "It bothers the hell out of us." You see, if sales management has challenging, stretch standards, doesn't it stand to reason that all sales personnel would not be able to attain such performance levels?

Of course it does!

*When sales manage-
ment has had no
management generated
turnover, it suggests
someone has lowered
the standards so that
everyone fits.*

When sales management has had no supervisory level generated turnover it suggests that sales management has lowered their standards so that everybody fits.

That's a non-manager and neither the sales manager nor his sales personnel are going to make it.

The Policeman:

In many cases the second way in which we might perceive our manager, almost the complete opposite of the NON-MANAGER, is more prevalent. This image is one of POLICEMAN.

Laborious call reports are mandatory yet all know they are seldom reviewed, if ever. Sales representatives of POLICEMEN at times are required to make physical appearances at the office to start each day or they are required to do likewise each evening prior to ending the work day. The manager seems to need to feel-touch-or-smell his sales-people to know that they are working.

*If we perceive
management to be
a policeman, all
communication stops.*

To a degree the sales manager's activities are related to that of a "spy." The salesperson may be required to phone the office to "check in" at frequent intervals, more for the reason of policing the salesperson than to receive communiques or information.

The result of perceiving your manager to be a POLICEMAN is you will withhold communication. You will resist submitting an itinerary, a work plan, because it is the salesperson's belief that the document is to "checkup-on-them." To spy on them. Depending on the degree of your perception of the manager as a POLICEMAN, a salesperson could almost function with a policy of *tell him nothing.* Again neither the sales manager nor the sales representative can perform in such an arena. Both will be in trouble. Both will fail to attain realistic goals because in such a circumstance all communication has ceased.

Clark Kent Identity

The most common image of the salesperson's line manager is that of "Clark Kent." Superman in disguise.

Working together in the field this type sales manager inevitably "takes over the

It is the salesman's responsibility to discover the customers needs. It is management's responsibility to uncover the salesman's needs.

sale!" He has house accounts. He receives direct phone calls from the customers and solves their problems one after another without involving his salesperson until after he has saved the day. He in fact is not a sales manager. He is a super-salesman who continues to do what his salespeople should be doing...sell!

If this is your image of your sales manager then again you both are in trouble. The salesperson is in fact as good as they are ever going to be. There will be no improvement because when challenging situations develop, the sales rep will step aside and the manager will be asked to enter and "save the day!" A *superman* manager work-relationship for salespeople is disastrous. The fact remains there is only one way people learn...they learn *by doing* and there is no other way. Superman sales managers are counter productive to the development of a skilled, competent sales team.

The Coach

The role of the sales manager, and how the salesperson should perceive them, is that of a "coach."

They train, they discipline, they establish standards...they coach.

They challenge the salespeople to perform at the maximum level of their capability...they may or may not be as good a salesperson as their subordinates but they know the systems, they are capable of teaching and they are capable of critique.

The professional salesperson would without question deliver an itinerary to a "coach" identified sales manager even if the itinerary was blank. The incompleted work plan would be the salesperson's method of communicating he or she needs help. Such a blank document would never be offered the policeman.

Some years ago one of the NFL professional football teams found themselves three points behind in the closing seconds of a critical game. This team had the ball, with only seconds to play on their opponent's one yard line and a decision had to be made.

Should the quarterback call for a field goal and tie the game?

Should he run or pass to win, and perhaps, be unsuccessful and lose?

His decision was to call time out and rush to the side line and his coach. Approaching the coach, the quarterback excitedly asked,

"Coach, what-d'ya-wanta-do?"

Well, point one...the coach did not grab the ball, run out on to the field and himself attempt to score.

Point two...he also did not direct the quarterback to run a quarterback sneak over the tackle. If he had, the quarterback would have raced back onto the field exclaiming,

"Boy, I sure hope it works because if it doesn't the *coach* is in really big trouble."

What actually happend was, almost immediately following the quarterback's request for direction:

"Coach, what-d'ya-wanta-do?"

The coach screamed,

"SCORE...dammit!" and the coach unbelievably walked away.

With sixty thousand fans yelling at the top of their lungs the realization of his accountability became quite clear. With

PEOPLE RARELY SUCCEED AT ANYTHING UNLESS THEY HAVE FUN DOING IT.

the coach disappearing in the mass of players the quarterback's responsibility was undeniable. His own thoughts excitedly to himself were:

IF IT
IS TO BE

IT IS
UP TO ME

Dick Beveridge, Jr.
and Associates

When management functions in a 'coaching capacity' and the salespeople feel a "crisis-to-perform," the team is almost unbeatable.

Aim So High You'll Never Be Bored

The
greatest waste
of our
natural resources
is the
number of
people
who never
achieve their
potential.
Get out
of that
slow lane.
Shift
into that
fast lane.
If you think
you can't,
you won't.
If you think
you can,
there's a
good chance
you will.
Even making
the effort
will make
you feel
like a new
person.
Reputations
are made
by searching
for things that
can't be done
and doing them.
Aim low:
boring.
Aim high:
soaring.

A message as published in the *Wall Street Journal*
by United Technologies Corporation, Hartford, Connecticut 06101

MAKING IT
HAPPEN VI

PART VI
MAKING IT
HAPPEN

To this point the techniques and skills of third and fourth generation salespeople are evident. There are some differences. There are real identifiable "uniquenesses" that result in a kind of competitive advantage over first and second generation types.

To guarantee the sales representative trends toward the more desirable skills, most professionals utilize "self-monitoring" tools. The "Trends Checklist" illustration provides the opportunity for such self-analysis.

Management functions as a reminder to the professional as to what additional skills he or she must acquire but management cannot do it alone. The sales professionals have their own self-motivated system of tracking their development and performance. We suggest this tracking is a great deal more than monitoring the pace toward established quantified and qualified sales targets. It is also the consistent tracking of the identified mandatory *skills* of the professional salesperson.

A Training Guide and Checklist can provide the needed measurement as detailed in illustration 6.1 and 6.2.

In our illustration titled Charles W. Williams this salesperson begins by manually entering his annual sales objective of $100,000 in the extreme left-hand column. It is understood that the more sophisticated companies provide this same information on monthly computer print outs. A greater awareness, however, results when the salesperson is disciplined to manually, each month, enter his actual sales figures. He can then accumulatively track his pace toward the attainment of that objective.

The value of the Training Guide and Checklist, however, is the direction it provides when the salesperson finds himself or herself behind the desired pace.

Professional sales types also have mandatory established goals as discussed previously in terms of their "PRODUCT MIX." Each year they will list the products in their line as detailed in our illustration and establish mandatory goals for each of these products. Should a salesperson find themselves behind the pace toward the attainment of the annual sales objective they scan this product-mix listing to determine which products they are *not* selling. Corrective activities can then result.

Should the sales rep be below target in both the pace toward an annual objective and in most products as well, they must evaluate their Training Guide and Checklist for their MARKET PENETRATION.

Again, in this extreme right-hand column as detailed in the illustration, the salesperson has at the year's beginning listed each of the classes of trade, the types of businesses that are the primary prospects for his or her products and/or services. They then as with their product-mix goals set out realistic, attainable, stretch, mandatory goals for each of the listed types of businesses. The evaluation is to determine what kinds of businesses they are not selling and to penetrate those markets as well.

So, to this point we are cognizant of the fact that professional salespeople do not measure their performance by how much they earn, nor by their activities but by their results.

GOAL ATTAINMENT STANDARDS . . . training guide and checklist.

SALES REPRESENTATIVE: CHARLES W. WILLIAMS
CITY CHICAGO **TERRITORY** #105 **YEAR** 82 FIRST QUARTER **GENERAL MGR.**

PERFORMANCE EVALUATION GRADE

Prev. Year	1st Qtr.	2nd Qtr.	3rd Qtr.	4th Qtr.
MM				

RE – Rarely Equaled   CE – Clearly Exceeds   MR – Meets Requirements   MM – Meets Minimum   FM – Fails To Meet

SALES MANAGER REVIEW DATES

1-6-82 2-10-82 3-9-82

Annual Sales $ Goal $100,000

Month	Percent		
Total			
12 Dec.			
11 Nov.			
10 Oct.			
9 Sept.			
8 Aug.			
7 July			
6 June			
5 May			
4 Apr.	287	27,135	28%
3 Mar.	178	16,507	
2 Feb.	8%		
1 Jan.			

Product Mix

Products	Annual Goal	Quarterly Actual	%
Word Processors	20,000	4,135	20%
Voice Recorders	25,000	1,500	6%
Transcribers	15,000	1,800	12%
Remote Systems	15,000	9,000	60%
Paper Stocks	10,000	7,500	75%
Accessories	15,000	3,200	21%

4th Qtr 75%   3rd Qtr 50%   2nd Qtr 25%   1st Qtr

Special Projects: FUNCTION AS FIELD TRAINER FOR NEW HIRES FIRST SIX MONTHS —1982

Performance Evaluation

Market Penetration

Type Business	Annual Goal	Quarterly Actual	%
Retail	30,000	11,585	38%
Mfg.	7,000	900	13%
Service	8,000	1,200	15%
Trans.	12,000	1,450	12%
Steel	6,000	600	10%
Electronic	33,000	11,400	35%

Other Information: TO COMPLETE "MAKING CUSTOMERS WANT TO BUY" SALES TRAINING PROGRAM prior to June '82

Fig. 6.1

SKILL STANDARDS . . . training guide and checklist.

(A) CUSTOMER MIX RESULTS
standard: 50% of calls to be on major size accounts. 35% on medium size acct

(B) SELLING TOOL USAGE
(Proposals - Brochures) Sales Case - Other)
standard: Must have independent awareness of contacts all brochures; Use yellow-felt marker to highlight customer needs areas; Proposals not price oriented.

(C) PROSPECTING
(Leads self generated - system functioning)
standard: 15 to 20% of planned time to be spent calling on wholly new accounts. Annually 3% of existing accounts to be handled and/or opened.

(D) PLANNING
(Itineraries - Territory Coverage - Goal Attainment Pace)
standard: Will submit 2 weekly work plan with both the name of the account and the objective of the call. To develop? Profile by 3rd quarter 1982.

(E) PRODUCT KNOWLEDGE
(Services - Features - Benefits - Usage)
standard: Will emphasize the companies systems, as opposed to individual products' hype and will know both products and applications of same in depth.

(F) ADMINISTRATION
(Reports - Factual Competitive Info - Sales Planning Sheets)
standard: Fill magazines provided Friday following week; Trip Guide; check list up to date consistently; Prospecting system functioning.

(G) ORGANIZATION
(Automobile - Sales Case - Time)
standard: Utilize a systematic approved itinerary coverage system; Selling tools available and both vehicle and personnel activities business like

(H) SELLING SKILLS
(Counselor Selling Skills)
standard: Evolutionary process to continue resulting in 'counselor' type abilities by 1-1-83.

(I) PERFORMANCE
(Total Sales - Product Mix - Market Penetration)
standard: MM evaluations in both skills and Goal Attainment awards for the entire year.

(J) DEVELOPMENT
(Job Improvement - Personal Growth - Increased Ability)
standard: To commence reviewing How to Lead and Motivate training program - fall 1982

(K) ATTITUDE
(Takes Direction - Commitment to Performance - Desire)
standard: Will be perceived as an 'orchestrator' by the company departments before June 1982

(L) OTHER 'ANALYSIS SKILLS'
Has accountability for competitor 'X'. Will evaluate all systems, techniques, products, problem, strengths, personnel and provide written dossier by Sept. 82

DWB – Sales 10

Fig. 6.2

The annual sales-target-pace results; the product-mix-goals results; and, the targets for each of the classes-of-trade who are prospects for his or her products or services.

It's possible that a salesperson could find themselves behind pace in all three categories. Behind in the attainment of their annual goal, behind in one or more of their product mix objectives and below pace in selling to selected markets.

If this is the case a review of the *skills* mandatory to selling is in order.

One or more of the skills may have been deleted. Planning? Prospecting? Organization? Administration? Selling tool usage?

Selling skills themselves? At this point the third or fourth generation professionals carefully review their standards and their meeting of the standards for each of the needed selling skills.

This listing is shown in the lower portion of the illustration. Our salesperson with sales management's guidance has determined what selling skills are mandatory for sales success in their industry. They are listed. Standards for each are agreed upon. i.e., the frequency at which itineraries will be prepared; the desired level of selling skill preferred, etc.... and with each in-the-field, on-the-job visitation of sales management both the "goal attainment" *and* the "skills development" are monitored, critiqued and evaluated by the sales manager.

The TRAINING GUIDE AND CHECKLIST when incorporated as a continuing component in the professional salesperson's arsenal provides a "mirror" of themselves. It functions as an interested, empathetic, silent sales manager...on guard, on site, on-your-side.

TEN TRENDS IN SELLING PROFESSIONALLY

This entire book promised not to tell salespeople "how-to-sell." It did promise to detail a profile of selling professionally as it is today. The actions if any which take place following the reading of the book will be determined by the salesperson's honest answer to the question...

HOW WILL I DO IN MY TERRITORY IF IT IS THE COMPETITOR'S SALES REPRESENTATIVE WHO IS DOING THESE THINGS?

Totally then it would seem there are emerging ten basic guidelines or factors in the *evolution of selling skills.* Recognizing that such skills are in a constant state of change even this list will be in an evolutionary state.

Trend One:
Professional sales types seem to have the ability to maintain purchasing agents in an administrative capacity, rarely allowing them to function in a "decision making" capacity. The contact is made with the P.A., but the professional sales type is able to go around him and get his

Purchasing agents are retained in an administrative capacity.

or her systems sold to those persons who are more interested in problem solving than price.

Trend Two:
The proposals of the professional are much more sophisticated. Although such proposals contain specifications and pricing information they are more descriptive of, and more oriented towards a detailing of the cutomer's identified needs and the systems and solutions to satisfy those needs.

Proposals are needs oriented.

Trend Three:
Rarely if ever will today's emerging top sales producers allow a supplier, staff person or sales manager to sell for them. They have an acute awareness of the need to be continually developing their own selling skills and an understanding that they will only learn such skills by "doing" and by being adequately and continuously 'coached.'

Entrepreneurs do not allow others to sell for them.

Trend Four:
You will seldom see the best salespeople sell or talk 'product' on the *initial*

They never sell on the initial sales call.

sales call. They recognize the objective is to uncover customer needs and to exit with an identity of problem solver and with an image of credibility. To immediately launch into a product 'pitch' establishes only a one-way dialog, which is amateurish.

Trend Five:

The professional salesperson's income is more than adequate and they are able to enjoy the good things in life. It is an unusual circumstance to uncover a professional however who tracks his or her performance or measures his or her performance by how much they earn.

Professional salespeople do not measure their performance by how much they earn.

They do not. Their measurements are more indicative of penetrating their markets effectively and that is always based on the potential of their territory.

Trend Six:

They tell the customer what they need.

A skilled salesperson would lose 'face' or a degree of pride in their competence if they were to categorically list their product line and ask their client to select what he or she wants. The professional demonstrates empathy, expertise and problem-solving skills by consistently *telling* their customers what *they need.*

Trend Seven:

Today's productive salespeople recognize they do not have the luxury of yesteryear when it was acceptable to negatively talk about, verbally voice objections about the competence of, and to "be-agin'" the other departments in the company. Today the salesperson believes he or she is the orchestrator, thinks as an orchestrator and functions as the liaison to orchestrate the needs of the customer with the capabilities of the company for which they sell.

They are team players.

Trend Eight:

Clearly, concisely, without any doubt...one of the most identifiable trends is the fact the professional understands they will rarely, long term, ever have a competitive advantage in product or price. In the thinking of today's sales professional their company's competitive advantage is in fact, themselves.

They understand their competitive advantage should be themselves.

A mandatory goals attitude.

Trend Nine:
They have a "I-must-make-it-happen" mandatory goals attitude. The professional knows very well that each year, every year there will be a logical, justifiable reason for not attaining the goal. A professional seems to be above most of these 'crutches' and functions with a determination to achieve "in-spite-of."

Trend Ten:
They, the most outstanding producers, insure they are in fact, in a constant state of challenge.

Are You?

SELLING THE SYSTEM WITH A CUSTOMER FOCUS

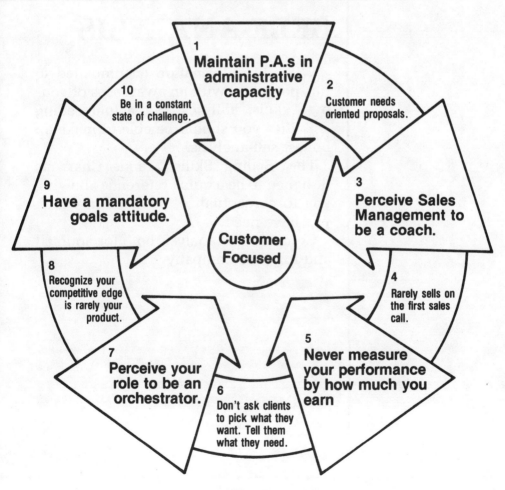

1 Maintain P.A.s in administrative capacity

2 Customer needs oriented proposals.

3 Perceive Sales Management to be a coach.

4 Rarely sells on the first sales call.

5 Never measure your performance by how much you earn

6 Don't ask clients to pick what they want. Tell them what they need.

7 Perceive your role to be an orchestrator.

8 Recognize your competitive edge is rarely your product.

9 Have a mandatory goals attitude.

10 Be in a constant state of challenge.

Customer Focused

Fig. 6.3

SELF-ANALYSIS

With the information accumulated to this point and with an awareness of your own skills, abilities and actual selling activities you should be able to make an honest self-analysis.

The 'Selling Skills Trends Chart' is designed to be a quick reference allowing you to perceptualize the areas in which you have need.

Complete the analysis both for yourself and for your company.

SELLING SKILLS 'TRENDS' CHART
INDIVIDUAL ANALYSIS

Consider each level carefully. Be honest with yourself. When ready, place an arrow, pointed left or right, in the shaded portion of each subject area as your assessment as to which way you are trending.

Yesterday Sales Types	Enter arrow to indicate direction you are trending.	Today Sales Types
Product Orientation		Needs Emphasis
Good Service Verbalizations		Demonstrations of Expertise
Single Product Emphasis		Systems Oriented
Internally Motivated		External Empathy
Quotes & Bids (price orientation)		Proposals (problem solving oriented)
Measures Activities		Measures Results
Goals are Targets or Guidelines		Goals are Mandatory
Asks Customer To pick what he wants		Tells Customer what he needs
Condemns support Groups		Team selling psychology

Now that you have evaluated yourself, repeat the process as an assessment of your company on the following page.

Fig. 6.4

SELLING SKILLS 'TRENDS' CHART
COMPANY ANALYSIS

Consider each level carefully. Be honest with yourself. When ready, place an arrow, pointed left or right, in the shaded portion of each subject area as your assessment as to which way you are trending.

Yesterday Sales Types	Enter arrow to indicate direction you are trending.	Today Sales Types
Product Orientation		Needs Emphasis
Good Service Verbalizations		Demonstrations of Expertise
Single Product Emphasis		Systems Oriented
Internally Motivated		External Empathy
Quotes & Bids (price orientation)		Proposals (problem solving oriented)
Measures Activities		Measures Results
Goals are Targets or Guidelines		Goals are Mandatory
Asks Customer To pick what he wants		Tells Customer what he needs
Condemns support Groups		Team selling psychology

Now that you have evaluated yourself, repeat the process as an assessment of your company.

Fig. 6.4

THREE KEY
CONSIDERATIONS
FOLLOWING YOUR ANALYSIS

1. Where, in terms of skills, are you today?

2. Where is it you have at this point determined you need
to be?

3. When is it you plan to be there?

WHERE IN TERMS OF SKILLS
AM I TODAY?

1.

2.

3.

4.

5.

6.

7.

8.

WHERE IS IT I
NEED TO BE?

1.

2.

3.

4.

5.

6.

7.

8.

WHEN DO I PLAN TO BE THERE?

GOAL	TARGET DATE

1.

2.

3.

4.

5.

6.

7.

8.

VIDEO TRAINING SYSTEMS FEATURING DON BEVERIDGE TO DEVELOP THESE SKILLS

HOW TO LEAD AND MOTIVATE SALES REPRESENTATIVES

Six dynamic hours of DON BEVERIDGE presentations providing the HOW TO of effective sales management. The program additionally includes an audio cassette tape series, training manuals, sales management tools and framed, signed certificates of completion. The best sales management training available!

HOW TO MAKE CUSTOMERS WANT TO BUY

A complete in-house sales training program presented by DON BEVERIDGE on six full hours of video tapes. The skills, the disciplines, the tools, the techniques and the motivation of the professional salesperson. Increased sales at improved profits are a direct result of this program's usage.

Write for Beveridge Business Systems descriptive brochures on these highly acclaimed developmental training programs. Send your request to:
Beveridge Business Systems
P.O. Box 223
Barrington, IL 60010